Patterns of
Wealthholding

In Wisconsin Since 1850

Patterns of Wealthholding

In Wisconsin Since 1850

Lee Soltow

University of Wisconsin Press

Madison, Milwaukee, and London

Published 1971
The University of Wisconsin Press
Box 1379, Madison, Wisconsin 53701

The University of Wisconsin Press, Ltd.
70 Great Russell Street, London, WCIB 3BY

First printing

Printed in the United States of America
Cushing-Malloy, Ann Arbor, Michigan

ISBN 0-299-05530-2; LC 77-101506

Contents

List of Exhibits

List of Tables

Preface

The quantitative differences in wealth between low, middle, and high income groups in a society can be of great interest. The differences are not merely reflections of the demand and supply of particular talents of given individuals in a technological arena. Rather, they are reflections of the many institutions of society which, in one way or another, allow economic disparities to arise and to be perpetuated. Farm land distribution policy, inheritance laws, differences in education, and the organizational procedures for individual and group work and pooling of capital are examples of independent variables affecting a dependent variable such as the distribution among people of wealth or income.

The most interesting aspect of wealth and income distribution is the possibility of its change over time, particularly over a long period. A quantification of distribution changes is a quantification of all the institutional and technological changes, and particularly of their impacts on different social classes. If one could obtain an index of distribution changes from the beginning of a society, he might better understand the importance of each institution among differing classes within the society. He might better judge the relative importance of each institution to society as a whole at different stages of development.

This book is a study of distribution changes in Wisconsin, for which wealth and income data are available for nearly the entire period of settlement. Information comes from the 1850, 1860, 1870, 1940, 1950, and 1960 censuses; the federal income tax returns from 1864 to 1869 and after 1916; estate and inheritance taxes for 1900, 1927, 1936, and after 1960; and the Wisconsin individual income tax returns after 1912. These sources permit one to obtain a rather complete coverage from the time of statehood in 1848 to the present.

The earliest comprehensive wealth data available for different economic groups in the United States are for the census year of 1860. In

that year, as well as in 1870, each individual was asked to state the
value of his real and personal estate. A more limited question pertaining to the value of real estate was asked in the 1850 census. These
1850—70 data are extremely valuable because they permit classification by the age, sex, occupation, nativity, and area of residence of the
wealthholder. If one wished to cover the complete history of a land
area from its frontier days and were limited by historical data to a period from 1850, he might well choose Wisconsin, a territory and state
with a population of 31,000 in 1840, 305,000 in 1850, 776,000 in 1860,
and 1,055,000 in 1870.[1]

The study of Milwaukee County within the context of the Wisconsin
analysis is particularly fruitful because it allows for urban-rural or
farm—non-farm contrasts and comparisons. In 1860 the county had 8
per cent of the adult male population. In 1960 it had 27 per cent. The
number of farms per adult in the county in 1860 was the same as that
in the state in 1960. The development of the county is an exaggeration
of the development in the state. Milwaukee County has some unique
data which have not been so readily available until very recently for
other cities. The incomes of all persons paying income tax were printed
in the *Milwaukee Sentinel* for the years 1865—69. Of these, the 1864
income data of the top 10 per cent of the male labor force will be given
some prominence in this study. The incomes of persons in the years
1913 and 1929, obtained from the Wisconsin individual income tax returns, are quite exceptional. They provide data for a relatively high
income area early in the century. The 1929 distribution, with relatively
low exemption levels as compared to federal returns, will be employed
extensively. In addition to these income distributions, one has a distribution of estates, essentially for Milwaukee County in the year 1900,
which was obtained from an investigation by Dr. Max Lorenz. These
figures are very important in trying to understand the period of industrialization from the Civil War to the turn of the century. Some attention is given to a complete census of mortgage values made from 1880
to 1890 not only in Milwaukee but in the rest of the state as well.

Chapter 1 includes a general summary of findings. The main investigation of the book is contained in Chapters 2, 3, and 4; it deals with
the censuses of wealth in 1850, 1860, and 1870. Chapter 2 includes
a description of the definitions, procedures, and limitations of the study
data and a detailed analysis of the 1860 wealth distribution in Milwaukee. The study is broadened to include an analysis of all 58 counties
in the state in 1860 in Chapter 3 (two of these counties had so few
residents that they were not always included in the analyses). Less
detailed results for 1850 and 1870 are given in Chapter 4. Chapter 5
is an attempt to compare the well-being of various nativity groups;
special reference is made to Norwegians, using some income and wealth
distribution data for Norwegians living in southern Norway and Nor-
wegian-born Wisconsin residents. Chapter 6 highlights distributions
after 1870. Changes in institutions affecting, and affected by, wealth

in the century are explored; they include inheritance or estate transmission, migration coupled with age-nativity changes, land settlement,
and education. A short income supplement pertaining to Milwaukee
and Wisconsin incomes is offered as Chapter 7. Emphasis is placed
on 1864 income tax data.

I wish to thank my wife for helping me with my manuscript in so
many ways. The study which has resulted in this publication was sup-
ported largely by a grant from the National Science Foundation. Strong
support also was given by Ohio University in the form of a reduced
teaching schedule and funds for initial investigation. However, the
conclusions, opinions, and other statements in this publication are
mine.

Athens, Ohio   *Lee Soltow*
Sept., 1969

Patterns of
Wealthholding

In Wisconsin Since 1850

Chapter 1

Introduction

A. THE PROBLEM

It is commonly believed that the relative share of wealth and income of the rich in the United States increased during the last half of
the nineteenth century and perhaps until as late as the end of World
War I. Reasons offered in support of this thesis of increased inequality
include the whole movement toward industrialization, with its concur-
rent developments of increasing urbanization, of factories, corporations,
financiers, robber barons, and laboring classes, which is contrasted to
the earlier agrarian economy. It is alleged that before 1890, and particularly before the Civil War, there was an era of homogeneous agrar-
ianism with an expanding frontier of free land. The belief that there
was relatively little ante-bellum inequality in the northern states is
crucial to the thesis. If there had been great inequality of land holdings similar to that in Great Britain, then movement toward industrialization might actually have left the rich with smaller relative gains than
those of the poor.[1] Certain doubts about the thesis arise when one
studies the history of the nineteenth-century United States.[2]

One issue not to be explored in this book is the abolition of slavery.
The confiscation of personal property in the form of slaves, the transfer of the ownership of human wealth to its rightful holders, was a very
important step toward economic as well as personal equality. The al-
lied issue of human acculturation and assimilation, which will be explored, pertains to the efficiency of land settlement. It is obvious that
a person did not land in New York one day and sell crops from eighty
acres on the next day. Even if he and all those like him were able to
do so, there still exists the problem of timing and economic growth.

An initial state of perfect equality of wealth becomes disturbed if
population, including immigration, expands greatly and individual wealth
accumulation proceeds at a rapid rate. Suppose that both on the ex-

treme frontier and in cities the former is 5 per cent and the latter is
7 per cent per annum. One who had lived in the United States for sixty
years, or who was fortunate enough to have inherited the accumulation
of his native-born father or grandfather, would find himself in a very
select economic group compared to those just beginning the American
experience. The population at any point in time would have great inequality provided that economic growth had taken place. Merle Curti's
absorbing book, *The Making of an American Community*, dealing with
the rural county of Trempealeau in western Wisconsin indicates that a
general analysis of the whole of Wisconsin would be an admirable
choice for the study of inequality. Comparisons for up to 58 counties,
including Milwaukee County, allow an analysis of inequality and economic growth for a wide spectrum of individuals and areas in the state.

One can test the inequality thesis only by examining available data.
As indicated in the preface, excellent data exist in the lists for the
United States of each individual and his declaration of the value of his
holdings, available from the 1850, 1860, and 1870 censuses. Since
such a census has never again been taken, they are the main source of
data; they can be supplemented for later years only by using data concerning the estates of deceased. Essentially, incomes of taxpayers
are available only for high income groups in the 1860's and after 1912
and will not be given much prominence in this book. Thus data are
available for the ante-bellum period to test the inequality thesis.

B. THE FINDINGS FOR 1860 WEALTH

The census of wealth for 1860 will be highlighted in this study. In
it wealth was defined as real estate plus personal estate. Very briefly,
real estate was reported wherever it was owned.[3] The individual decided whether or not he wished to subtract debt. Personal estate value
was defined as including all bonds, stock, mortgages, notes, livestock,
plate, jewels, or furniture, but excluding wearing apparel. Aggregates
for northern states were published and appear to be in excellent accord
with backward extrapolations and interpolations of data of Professors
Raymond W. Goldsmith, Simon Kuznets, and Richard Easterlin.[4] We shall
consider findings for wealth averages and wealth inequality, using six
classifications: (1) for Wisconsin, (2) for Milwaukee County, (3) for
all counties in Wisconsin, (4) for Wisconsin occupational groups,
(5) for Wisconsin age-nativity groups, and (6) for Milwaukee County
age-nativity groups.

1. A sample of every twentieth person was drawn from Wisconsin's
population in 1860. The wealth distribution for the state's 200,000
adult males 20 years and over encouragingly had no discontinuities. A
succinct table showing its large spread is:

Lower class limit	Frequency	Share of total wealth
$ 0 –	0.288	0.000
1 –	.355	.093
1,000 –	.338	.609
10,000 –	.019	.248
100,000 –	.0004	.050
	1.000	1.000

The median was $350 and the arithmetic mean was $1,500. The Gini coefficient of inequality,[5] R, was 0.75.

The average wealth of $1,500 (approximately $5,000 in terms of 1960 prices) was surprisingly high for an area which had been a state for only 12 years. Even more startling was the dispersion from this average. Almost 30 per cent of the men were essentially propertyless, 40 per cent had less than $200, and 50 per cent had less than $350. At the other end of the curve were 86 individuals who had wealth above $100,000: they held 5 per cent of the total wealth of the 200,000 men. The top 2 per cent held 31 per cent of total wealth. Even though these figures show wide disparity, one may wonder whether it is greater than that in the 1960's. Robert Lampman, admittedly using very different definitions, found that the top 2 per cent of families in the United States held 33 per cent of wealth in 1922 and 29 per cent in 1953.[6] A Federal Reserve study of consumer unit heads in the United States in 1962 gave a wealth distribution[7] with a Gini coefficient, or R, of 0.76. Our coefficient for Wisconsin in 1860 was 0.75.

2. Milwaukee County, with 8 per cent of the men in the state in 1860, exhibited even greater relative inequality among its 15,900 men.

Lower class limit	Frequency	Share of total wealth
$ 0 –	0.336	0.000
1 –	.415	.051
1,000 –	.207	.266
10,000 –	.039	.427
100,000 –	.0030	.256
	1.000	1.000

In this case the median was $100, the mean was $2,400, and R was 0.89. Interestingly, the 33 per cent who were propertyless represented only 5 more per hundred than the 28 per cent propertyless for the state. This extreme inequality came about essentially because, of the more than 15,000 men in the county, the 46 richest men held over 25 per cent of total wealth: the top 2 per cent held over 50 per cent of the total wealth. The top 2 per cent in Milwaukee owned the equivalent of 7 per cent of the state's total wealth.

The 46 top wealthholders had a median age of 45 and were largely persons born in the East, half of them in the state of New York. Their occupations were banker, real estate dealer, lawyer, lumber merchant, or general merchant. In any case, their economic power was tremendous considering the fact that Milwaukee land had first been offered for sale only 25 years earlier.

3. Average wealth varied substantially from county to county in Wisconsin. Area inequality, computed from the assumption that each individual in a county had wealth equal to that of the average wealth for the county, gave an R of 0.19 for the state. This was 26 per cent of the state's overall Gini R of 0.75. It is not surprising that the degree of urbanization, or density, among counties was important. An analysis was made of the relationship between the average wealth per adult male in a county, or W, and the number of persons per square mile in each county, or D, for the 56 effective counties in 1860. Averages were highest in the denser counties in the southeastern part of the state. The logarithmic regression equation for the 44 counties in 1860 with density greater than 4 per square mile was $W = \$660\ D^{0.2}$. Population increased 10 per cent per year in Wisconsin from 1850 to 1860 and one may assert with some reasonableness that $D = 1.10^t$, where t is time in years. Combination of these equations yields $W = \$660\ (1.020)^t$. Thus there is the implication that average per capita wealth was increasing 2 per cent a year in this period. The 12 counties with density less than 4 per square mile, the counties at the frontier, disappointingly had widely fluctuating averages. Their population was, of course, a very small per cent of the total for the state.

It was found from an analysis of the 44 counties that the cash value of farms per acre correlated well with wealth and that cash value was very strongly correlated with density. Using the same procedure as described above for wealth, leads to a 4.4 per cent per annum growth factor for land value. Inclusion of a land improvement factor possibly means that over half of this growth may be attributed to increased population and less than half to improvement of land.

A very laborious calculation was made of the inequality of wealth in each county, R. Classification by density, D, for each of the 56 counties gives:

Lower limit of R class	Density of the county			
	$D < 4$	$4 < D < 40$	$D > 40$	All
0.5 −		4		4
0.6 −	2	14	3	19
0.7 −	7	9	10	26
0.8 −	3	3	1	7
	12	30	14	56
Average R	0.76	0.68	0.72	0.71

There was a large range in R from 0.52 to the 0.89 value in Milwaukee

County. Very importantly, this was not particularly related to the development in the county. Most of the 12 counties with density under
4 persons per square mile were located in a band running west from
Green Bay, an area at the edge of fertile farm land and harsh growing
climate. The counties in the middle density group had less inequality
than those in the highest density group but the difference was not great.
Milwaukee County, with a density 4 times that of the next nearest
county, clearly was in a category by itself. The relatively dense counties surrounding it had inequality no larger than that in the state as a
whole. The correlation between R and D is weakly negative for all
56 counties and weakly positive for the top 44 counties. Thus, there
is no clear linear pattern. The 12 frontier counties had greater inequality but they could not be thought to constitute a proper agricultural
frontier because of climate and terrain. The inequality of land holdings, considering the number of persons who were propertyless, was
found to be highly correlated with wealth inequality. The proportion of
those without land on the frontier was relatively high and land inequality was inversely related to density.

  4. Let us consider another aspect of development for the state, the
occupational dichotomy of farmer (including farm laborer or hired hand)
and non-farmer. Among men in Wisconsin in 1860

	Frequency	Mean	R
Farmers	0.598	$1,590	0.69
Non-farmers	.402	1,340	0.83
All	1.000	1,490	0.75

The average wealth of non-farmers, interestingly, was near that of farmers and was actually larger among those in the age class from 30 to 50.
The difference in inequality, 0.69−0.83, might be thought to be extremely
important because of relative farm to non-farm population movement,
mainly to towns or cities.

Lower-class limit	Frequency among men in 1860		
	All	Farmers	Non-farmers
$ 0−	0.288	0.251	0.346
1−	.355	.309	.407
1,000−	.339	.427	.222
10,000−	.019	.013	.024
100,000−	.0004	.0001	.0010
	1.000	1.000	1.000

If the relative migration was toward the urban areas, then why didn't
inequality of wealth increase in the state over time from 0.75 to a larger
figure, such as 0.83? If one looks only at 1860 data, the explanation
would seem to depend on a study of age distributions. This is a key to

the effective use of manpower through time. The greatest inequality of
wealth among adult males lies in the age class 20—29. It then decreases until old age with a prevailing negative relationship between
age and inequality. The population of adult males aged substantially
after 1850. It is possible to demonstrate that lessened inequality from
age can counteract an increase in inequality because of urban movements.

5. There is an interesting pattern for wealth averages which appears
when data are classified by age and nativity for men in Wisconsin in
1860.

Age	All	Native born	Foreign born
20—29	$ 500	$ 630	$ 390
30—39	1,500	1,940	1,190
40—49	2,240	2,920	1,770
50—59	2,760	4,180	1,590
60—69	1,720	2,600	1,040
20—99	1,490	1,960	1,100

The exponential equation considering wealth, W, and age in years, A,
fitted to all cases in the Wisconsin sample is $W = \$7.15(1.078)^A$. A
man one year older than another in 1860 had, on the average, 7.8 per
cent more wealth. Among native born, the percentage was 8.8 for farmers and 9.5 for non-farmers. Among foreign born, it was 6.1 and 6.2.
The age-time implication is that persons experienced an average increase in wealth each year of about 8 per cent and that native born had
a growth rate almost half again as large as foreign born.

6. Another interesting pattern unfolds for Milwaukee County when
1860 wealth is classified by nativity for certain age ranges, particularly
those between ages 30 and 60. Moving averages show that wealth increases with age in a curvilinear fashion but that a linear ratio trend
allows one to make generalizations. It was found that the wealth of a
person one year older than another was, on the average, 8.3 per cent
higher among native born and 6.6 per cent higher among foreign born.
There is a very strong implication that the economic growth rate for an
individual was at least as high as these values. The idea of employing
age as a proxy for time is expanded at length in the text before assert-
ing that the apparent growth rates were an impressive 8.3 and 6.6 per
cent. It is also established that, in 1860, the native-born wealth for a
given age, A, was approximately the same as that for a foreign-born
wealth average of age $A + 30$, thus neatly leaving a gap of one generation.

The configuration is also found for population and age figures, with
an apparent growth rate for population of 5.3 per cent a year among foreign born and 6.3 per cent a year among native born. Again a lag of
about 30 years appears, with the number of foreign born at age $A + 30$

being the same as the number of native born at age A. This leads to the idea that the native-born per capita wealth ratio was 1.083/1.063, or 1.019, and that for foreign born was 1.066/1.053, or 1.013. Thus, the model in Milwaukee County was a staircase:

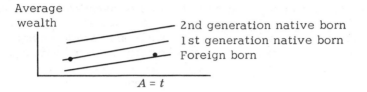

An examination of native-born groups in Wisconsin shows that the average wealth of those born in New York, Delaware, and New Jersey was over 3 times that of those born further west. This perhaps is a measure of being a first- or second-generation American.

C. THE FINDINGS FOR 1850 AND 1870 WEALTH

The six points given for 1860 will now be expanded to include changes over time. According to various censuses, Wisconsin's population of adult males grew from 12,000 in 1840 to 84,000, 199,000, and 265,000 in 1850, 1860, and 1870. There are no wealth data for 1840. The data for 1850 are only for real estate, fortunately about 80 per cent of total estate or wealth. The definition of wealth, including real and personal estate, was similar in 1860 and 1870.

1. The inequality coefficient for Wisconsin in 1850, 1860, and 1870 was (R:0.77, 0.75, 0.74), indicating that there was little change in inequality. This is quite remarkable when one considers that the population of adult males increased on the average 22, 9, and 3 per cent per annum in the three decades from 1840 to 1870. In 1850, real estate values were very unevenly held. Ten men had over 3 per cent of the value of the holdings of the 84,000 men in the state of that year. They included three merchants, two landowners, a lawyer, a banker, a blacksmith, a manufacturer. Their median age was 41; nine were born in the United States, seven in New York. Six lived in Milwaukee. These were the agrarian counterpart to the emerging industrial giants in 1870. The 1870 giants were in railroads, telegraphing, distilling, and threshing-machine manufacturing. The top 25 men in 1870 reported less than 2 per cent of total wealth in the state. Median wealth of all men in Wisconsin seems to have increased a little more rapidly than arithmetic mean wealth from 1850 to 1870. The whole phenomenon is inextricably connected with the aging of the population. The median age of males 20 and over in the state was 36 in 1850, 38 in 1860, and 40 in 1870. Age cohorts showed decreasing inequality from 1850 to 1870.

2. For Milwaukee County, there is evidence that inequality at worst remained the same, and at best decreased 5 to 10 per cent in the twenty years from 1850 to 1870. The value for R for real estate holdings of men was 0.91 in 1850 and 0.88 in 1860. Considering wealth or total estate, it was 0.89 in 1860 and 0.85 in 1870. Some few persons held immense areas of land compared to the two of every three men reporting no real estate value in 1850. By 1870, there was some evidence of a "tycoon effect" with one railroad executive and banker holding 0.4 per cent of wealth, or more than the total wealth of the lower half of the 22,000 males. In spite of this effect, middle groups probably gained relative to the upper groups. The poor young decreased in relative importance from 1860 to 1870.

3. Studies were made of the 31 counties in the state in 1850 and the 58 counties in 1870 which supplement the study of 56 measurable counties in 1860. The relationships between wealth and density indicate that per capita growth rates were very high, perhaps 8 per cent as reflected in the 1850 data, while being 2 per cent in 1860, and perhaps less than 2 per cent in 1870.

The inequality level, R, and density, D, were negatively related in all three years. In 1850, the ten counties with lowest density had Gini coefficients averaging 0.84; the middle ten averaged 0.76, and the eleven high density counties averaged 0.74. The curvilinear pattern found for 1860 was also found in 1870. The linear elasticity coefficients were (E_{RD}: -0.04, -0.01, -0.04).

The inequality level was positively related to wealth in 1860 but was inversely related in 1850 and 1870. (E_{RW}: -0.10, +0.05, -0.08). The county relationships, with but one exception in the three census years, were such that an increase in population density or an increase in average wealth was consistent with slight decreases in inequality.

4. The proportion of men in Wisconsin listing farming or farm labor as their occupation was consistent in definition only in 1860 and 1870:[8]

Year	Proportion in farming	Gini coefficient of wealth		
		Farmers	Non-farmers	All
1850	0.57	0.67	0.89	0.77
1860	0.60	0.69	0.83	0.75
1870	0.54	0.62	0.86	0.74

The results are somewhat mixed but they do demonstrate that the proportion in farming could increase or decrease while overall inequality decreased or remained constant. The 1860 and 1870 figures could mean that the pull of the non-farm sector might have caused decreased inequality in the farm sector at the same time that inequality was increased in the non-farm sector.

5. The positive correlation between wealth and age for men in Wisconsin surprisingly was weakest in 1850 and strongest in 1870. As an

example, the ratio of average wealth of those 40—49 compared to those 30—39 was (W_{40-49}/W_{30-39}: 1.15, 1.42, 1.43). A more elaborate measure of the same effect is the form $W = d(1+r)^A$ fitted to all cases in the three samples. This gives values of (r: 0.061, 0.078, 0.096). One interpretation is that in 1850 very few people had been in the state more than 10 years. Perhaps half of the men had not been there more than four years. The effect of economic growth might not be so firmly imbedded in age as it was 10 or 20 years later.

6. Milwaukee County in 1870 had somewhat the same wealth-age differential it had in 1860, with apparent growth rates for selected age classes of 7.8 per cent for native born and 4.4 per cent for foreign born. There were relatively fewer young, particularly young foreign born in 1870 as compared to 1860.

D. FINDINGS FOR WEALTH AFTER 1870

1. Estimates of broad aggregate wealth owned by all persons and public bodies in Wisconsin have been made for eight points in time by the census authorities from material from censuses from 1860 to 1922. These data indicate that this comprehensive wealth per adult male in Wisconsin increased 2 per cent a year during this period. There has been no Wisconsin census where the individual has been asked to state his wealth since the census of 1870.

2. We have the estates of deceased above certain filing levels for several years including those for Wisconsin in 1927—28 and 1963. It was decided that these could reasonably be compared to the estates of the living males 50 years old and over in 1860 above certain wealth levels. Our Gini coefficient cannot be used effectively since results are not available for the entire wealth range. It is necessary to resort to an established procedure for these upper tail distributions, a cumulative frequency curve or inverse-Pareto curve of the form $W = A (L_W)^{-b}$. In this form, L_W is the number of returns or persons with wealth above the value W. Greater inequality is shown by greater values of b. Estimates for b in 1860, 1927—28, and 1963 are 0.67, 0.68, and 0.66. One concludes that the relative inequality among the rich has not changed in Wisconsin since the time when it became a state. A 6.6 to 6.8 per cent decrease in the dollar wealth level is associated with a 10 per cent increase in the number of persons above this level in each of the three years.[9] Similarities between the results for Wisconsin in 1860 and the United States in 1922, 1953, and 1962 have been noted previously.

3. A similar procedure was followed for Milwaukee in comparing 1900 estates of deceased, essentially for that county, with 1860 values for the county above certain dollar minimums. The b in the inverse-Pareto form was 1.07 in 1860 and 0.93 in 1900. The value in 1900 shows less inequality than the value in 1860. The available 1900 distribution has

estimates for all deceased males so that Gini coefficients may also be computed. The value of R is 0.84 for deceased males in 1900 and 0.88 for males 50 and over in 1860.

4. Census data on every real estate mortgage recorded in Wisconsin and Milwaukee in each year from 1880 to 1889 were examined. These have bearing on gross wealth creation. The inequality coefficients remained remarkably constant in the decade for this sensitive part of wealth transfer and ownership. The growth in the number of lots mortgaged was nearly double the growth in the number of adult males. Ownership of lots in cities became an important counterpart to ownership of farms in the country.

5. An investigation of inheritances was made from data of the 1927–28 study. The recipients of transfers had an inverse-Pareto slope b of 0.699, almost the same as that of the original **estates** of 0.683, but a dollar wealth level only 70 per cent of that of the original estates. The inheritance mechanism left the inequality level among the rich the same as it was before the transfer. The beneficiaries, however, were a larger group than the decedents. This new elite group would have to accumulate for a period of years before its estimates would approach the size of the original estates.

6. Land distributions of the size of farms have been scrutinized for Wisconsin in selected years from 1860 to 1960. The value for R has decreased from about 0.40 in 1860 to less than 0.35 in 1960 while the number of farms per adult male has decreased to the point where it is no higher than it was in Milwaukee County a century ago.

One wonders anew how the distribution of wealth in 1860 might have had an R almost twice that of the distribution of land. A detailed study was made of the farm population of Milwaukee County in 1860 where land acreage had an R of 0.38 and wealth distribution of men had an R of 0.73. The gap between the two possibly could be explained as follows: **fertility** of land and proximity to the city gives an R of 0.44 for the value of farms. The addition of landless farm laborers and farmers with no land increases R substantially to 0.64. Multiple ownership of farms increases R to a value of 0.73.

7. Education could provide the beginning for youth that free land formerly provided. Evidence for Milwaukee indicates that from 1890, the average number of years of formal education has increased 1 per cent a year and that the inequality coefficient has been dramatically cut in half. In 1860, Milwaukee County had an adult male labor force which was 80 per cent foreign born. Today it has less than 8 per cent foreign born. The reduced immigration rate makes it possible for the young to have higher incomes than they otherwise might have had. They then can accumulate wealth as their elders have done.

8. The general conclusion is that wealth inequality, particularly among upper wealth groups, has changed very little in Wisconsin since its settlement. How could this happen in a state which originally had

free land? Various changes have been discussed: the purchase of urban real estate, the intergenerational transfers of property to an expanding population, and the decrease of dispersion in the amount of
education. One could also mention estate and inheritance taxes and
constraints on income inequality which have bearing on inequality of
wealth accumulation.

The basic reason, however, is that there was such large inequality
at the time of settlement. The need for large numbers of hired farm
laborers, the inefficiency in finding suitable land, and the large number
of poor foreign born left a large propertyless group at any point in time.
Strong economic growth meant that there were some rich native-born
families who, on the average, had been accumulating at a handsome rate
perhaps for several generations.

E. FINDINGS FROM THE INCOME SUPPLEMENT

The ownership of non-human wealth of an individual may very well
not reflect his income, particularly when he is young. Certain observations concerning incomes of persons have been made for those living in
Wisconsin and Milwaukee County in the last 100 years. The following
observations certainly are not exhaustive and are somewhat speculative
in nature.

1. The exponential trend fitted to census wage rates in manufacturing since 1860 yields for Milwaukee County $Y = \$244(1.018)^t$, where t
is zero in 1860, and Y is average wages in 1860 dollars. The rate for
Wisconsin is 2.1 per cent a year.

2. Analysis of day labor rates, DL, for 32 counties in 1860 indicates
that these rates were clearly higher at the frontier than they were in the
more densely populated areas of the southeastern part of the state. The
elasticity with respect to density, D, was $E_{DL,D} = -0.08$. A county with
10 per cent less density had, on the average, 8 per cent higher rates.
It might have been expected that labor rates were inversely correlated
with average wealth in the 32 counties. The elasticity was $E_{DL,W} =$
-0.22.

3. Incomes of upper income persons in Milwaukee County are available for the years 1863 to 1868. They all have approximately the same
Pareto slopes and the income year 1864 has been chosen for further
analysis because the proportion of the labor force paying a tax was the
highest in that year. The inverse-Pareto curve for 1864 for the top 10
per cent of the labor force was $Y = \$83(N_Y)^{-0.71}$, where N_Y is the pro-
portion of the total labor force above income Y adjusted to 1860 prices.
We might first compare this result to the inverse-Pareto curve in 1860
for the same proportion of wealthholders, where $W = \$829(N_W)^{-0.79}$.
Income inequality, as measured by b values, was 10 per cent less than
wealth inequality. The ratio of the actual mean income to actual mean
wealth for this top group was 7.2 per cent.

The 1864 curve also may be compared to inverse-Pareto curves in 1929 and 1959 for males in Milwaukee County. Very satisfying growth rates of about 2 per cent are obtained from the implicit arithmetic means of these curves extrapolated to cover the entire male labor force. The slopes were 0.71, 0.57, and 0.41 for the three years. The indication, from top income data, is that income inequality has been cut to 4/7 of its former level. Some Lorenz curves were established for all adult males in 1864 using various assumptions about incomes of individuals below the filing requirement, considering wage rates in manufacturing and day labor rates. This led to R values between 0.55 and 0.75 for the incomes of men in the county in 1864. The actual R for the incomes of men in the county in 1959 was 0.35.

Incomes for the top 5 per cent of men in Wisconsin in 1863 had a value for b of 0.58. Unfortunately we do not have another value until 1913 when b was 0.55. Values after 1913 show a long-run downward trend in equality, being 0.41 in 1962. We do not know what happened in the interval from the 1860's to after the turn of the century.

Chapter 2

Wealth Distribution
in Milwaukee in 1860

The United States censuses in the middle of the nineteenth century are of singular economic interest because each individual in each county was asked to declare his wealth in dollars; for the 1850 census wealth meant the real estate owned by the individual; in the 1860 and 1870 censuses wealth meant both the owned real and personal property. Probably the most valuable data are for 1860, since the definition was more comprehensive than in 1850 and because there was much less antagonism to the United States government in 1860 than in the decade of strong taxation which followed.[1] It is for these reasons that the data for 1860 will be featured.

Since this source of data is the most important in this book from an analytical point of view, several aspects will be considered, including methods of collection and strengths and weaknesses of the information. Some readers may wish to examine the first five sections of this chapter quickly. They deal with the source of information, definition of wealth, secrecy, obligations, sampling procedures, choice of microcomponent, and the problem of illegibility. It is at the end of these sections that we begin to analyze Milwaukee data as an introduction to our pursuit of inequality levels. Milwaukee data are presented before those for Wisconsin mainly because it is easier to comprehend and to identify economic characteristics in a smaller area.

A. ADEQUACY OF DATA

1. *Source of Information*

The illustration of Schedule 1 of the 1860 census shown in Exhibit 1 gives an excellent picture of the source of the available data. It will be noted that the age, sex, color, occupation, real and personal estate, and nativity of each individual in a township are given. The assistant

SCHEDULE 1.—Free Inhabitants in _____ in the County of _____ State of _____ enumerated by me, on the ___ day of _____ 1860. _____

Post Office _____

Dwelling-houses numbered in the order of visitation.	Families numbered in the order of visitation.	The name of every person whose usual place of abode on the first day of June, 1860, was in this family	Age	Sex	Color, (White, black, or mulatto.)	Profession, Occupation, or Trade of each person, male and female, over 15 years of age.	Value of Real Estate.	Value of Personal Estate.	Place of Birth, Naming the State, Territory, or Country.	Married within the year	Attended School within the year.	Persons over 20 y'rs of age who cannot read & write.	Whether deaf and dumb, blind, insane, idiotic, pauper, or convict.
		1	2	3	4	5	6	7	8	9	10	11	12	13	14
		Ann Bayley	2	F					Wisconsin				
		August	4½	M				Do				
		Peter Linck	21	M	Clerk			Hamburg				
476	476	William Frank	43	M	Shoe Maker	1000	50	England				
		Nancy R.	33	F				Do				
		Mary M.	9	M				Wisconsin				
		Eliza	6	M				Do				
		Emma	2	F				Do				
		Nathan	62	M				Do				
477	476	Carl C. Zeleman	31	M			100	Pennsylvania	1		
		Cecelia R.	21	M	Clerk			Do	1		
		Nathan H.	13	F				Do			
478		Lou	20	F	Servant			Germany			
477	477	Jacob Fick	45	M		8500	1000	New York			
		Sarah L.	36	F		3000		Do	1		
		Mary A.	11	F				Do			
		Carlos	9	M				Wisconsin	1		

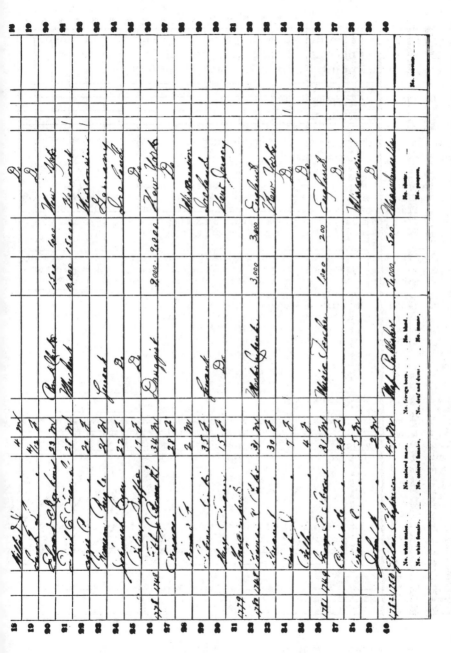

Example of Schedule 1 of the 1860 Census.   Courtesy of the Library of the State Historical Society of Wisconsin

17

marshals presumably made three copies of the schedules, one filed in
the county offices, one in the state offices, and one in Washington.
These last were microfilmed and made available to the general public
in the 1950's by the National Archives. An abridgment of the instructions governing the 1860 census appears in Appendix 1.

2. *Definition of Estate Owned*

We are concerned with the definition of real estate and personal estate and what the respondent considered in determining wealth value.
The 1860 instructions were

Value of Real Estate. Under heading 8, insert the value of real estate owned by each
individual enumerated. You are to obtain this information by personal inquiry of each
head of a family, and are to insert the amount in dollars, be the estate located where it
may. You are not to consider any question of lien or encumbrance; it is simply your duty
to enter the value as given by the respondent.

Value of Personal Estate. Under heading 9, insert (in dollars) the value of personal
property or estate. Here you are to include the value of all the property, possessions,
or wealth of each individual which is not embraced in the column previous, consist of
what it may; the value of bonds, mortgages, notes, slaves, live stock, plate, jewels, or
furniture; in fine, the value of whatever constitutes the personal wealth of individuals.
Exact accuracy may not be arrived at, but all persons should be encouraged to give a
near and prompt estimate for your information. Should any respondent manifest hesitation or unwillingness to make a free reply on this or any other subject, you will direct
attention to Nos. 6 and 13 of your general instructions and the 15th section of the law.
(See Appendix 1.)

In 1850, the instruction for item 8 was to

...obtain the value of real estate owned by each individual enumerated. You are to obtain the value of real estate by inquiry of each individual who is supposed to own real
estate, be the same located where it may, and insert the amount in dollars. No abate-
ment of the value is to be made on account of any lien or incumbrance thereon in the
nature of debt.

In 1870

Column 8 will contain the value of all real estate owned by the persons enumerated, with
out any deduction on account of mortgage or other incumbrance, whether within or without the census subdivision or the county. The value meant is the full market value know
or estimated.

Personal estate, column 9, is to be inclusive of all bonds, stock, mortgages, notes, live
stock, plate, jewels, or furniture, but exclusive of wearing apparel. No report will be
made when the personal property is under $100.[2]

The definitions seem to indicate that wealth data are totals before
subtraction of debt in 1850 and 1870 and in part in 1860. There is thus
a question of magnification of size. It will be shown, however, that

incomes net of expenses and gross wealth have a constant ratio through a wide range of data. A more difficult problem perhaps is the establishment of ownership. Suppose a land agent was holding large amounts of real estate for some eastern land-speculating group. He might or might not have rights to sell the land for the group. It is suspected that there are at least a few of these individuals whose real estate figures are very large. This can occur even though the agents personally have only very little or none of their own money invested in the group venture. Technically, then, one can insist on talking about the control of wealth rather than its ownership. It may be true in part that we are considering control over resources, but our statistical findings will give evidence that it is more likely to be ownership rights that are measured by the wealth data.

3. *Secrecy*

Of particular interest in establishing the validity of the wealth data of columns 8 and 9 of Exhibit 1 is whether the information was to be treated as confidential. An article from the *Cleveland Leader* in 1860 indicates that the questions to be asked were not even made public. The newspaper offered to publish a list of questions it had obtained if other people would do so, too. Marshals were forbidden from communicating the census findings to individuals for publication or any other purpose.[3]

Although copies of the original records were deposited with the clerks of the courts, the instructions indicate that it was not the intent that these records should be made available to "anyone" without a purpose. Unfortunately, there is no real information as to whether tax assessors had access to Schedule 1 in 1860. It was determined in Washington (supposedly in the 1940's) that the personal information of the census through 1880 (and those fragments for 1890 that survived the fire in 1921) could be made available for legitimate historical, geneological, and other, research. The records in the Library of the State Historical Society of Wisconsin were used at least as early as the 1920's.[4]

We still face the issue of whether it might have behooved an individual to declare an amount less than the actual value of his estate because of fear of tax authorities, or to declare an amount larger than actual value if he thought it would give him prestige or enhance the sale of assets at a good price. One imperfect check is to compare the totals obtained from Schedule 1 for individuals with those totals obtained from public records for the county. Let us define VEOI as the value of the estate owned by individuals as obtained from columns 8 and 9 of Schedule 1, VEOA as the value of the estate in the county as determined by assessors and reported in Schedule 6 of the census, and VEOT as the "true" value of the estate in the county as determined by an expert or the assistant marshal and reported in Schedule 6 of the census.

	1860 Milwaukee	1860 Wisconsin
VEOI	$38,712,145	$294,901,000
VEOA	15,984,000	185,944,000
VEOT	22,840,000	273,671,000

	1870 Milwaukee	1870 Wisconsin
VEOI	$65,875,000	$625,000,000
VEOA	51,275,000	333,209,000
VEOT	88,422,000	702,307,000

Note that the VEOI totals are very high relative to VEOA and VEOT totals for the year 1860. Part of this might be due to the fact that VEOI includes wealth owned "be the estate located where it may," while the VEOA and VEOT are limited to the county or state. In any case, a dramatic change took place from 1860 to 1870 in Milwaukee, when the VEOI/VEOT ratio was 3/4 instead of 1/1 or 2/1 as it had been in 1860. The VEOI/VEOA ratio also decreased radically. Probably individuals in 1860 stated more accurately their real wealth.

4. *Sampling Procedures*

To have taken a complete enumeration of individuals in Wisconsin or even Milwaukee County would have necessitated time and resources far in excess of those of the investigator. It was necessary to develop sampling procedures as the investigation progressed; these can be described in three main areas, namely, Milwaukee County, other counties in Wisconsin, and the state of Wisconsin. After investigating Milwaukee County, it was decided to investigate the rest of the state, obtaining at least some minimum detail by county. A difficulty from the standpoint of random sampling error is that a sample for a county might have to be almost as large as that for the state. It was decided to take two samples. One proceeded on a county-by-county basis, recording only positive information from items 8 and 9 on real and personal estate, but assuring a minimum size sample in each county. The other sample was drawn for the state at large considering, besides columns 8 and 9, all germane variables such as age, nativity, and occupation. The county-by-county sample for 1860 was five times as large as that of the state sample. The reader may feel that the two sample studies should have been combined into one study. The county study was designed to obtain each county wealth distribution as quickly as possible, obviating the use of IBM cards. The state sample reflected sample population densities. Low density areas were not sampled in a disproportionate fashion in the state study.

In the case of Milwaukee in 1860, data were obtained from a sample of 1 of every 20 males, 20 years old and over, whose estates were less than $20,000. A complete enumeration was made of those whose estates were over $20,000. This meant that one searched for every male

on each page. Every twentieth person was chosen for the sample unless his estate was more than $20,000. The cutoff of $20,000 was
used in Milwaukee as a preliminary guess of the 95th percentile; it
was actually closer to the 98th percentile. However, it was found that
more than 50 per cent of total wealth was accounted for by this cutoff
because of the extreme inequality of holdings. The total sample size
in Milwaukee was 1,092 items, of which 750 were below $20,000 and
342 above $20,000. This yields a male population of 15,342, slightly
less than the census count of 15,900 for that year.

A non-stratified sample for the state as a whole in 1860 will be presented in Chapter 3. Lines on the enumeration sheet were sampled in
order to obviate the onerous job of seeking each male 20 years old and
over. This introduced sampling error in the number of males 20 years
old and over. The number of adult males was 199,476/775,881, or approximately 25 per cent of the state's total population. If one wished
to have 1/20 of the males, 1/20 times 1/0.25, or 1 of every 5 lines
would be sampled. It was necessary to stagger the lines chosen on
each page because of the pattern occurring within a page (the first line
on a page would list the head of a household perhaps 80 per cent of the
time). A system was established whereby each of the 40 lines on the
left-hand enumeration sheet and the 40 lines on the right-hand enumeration sheet was sampled effectively with equal frequency. Results of
a stratified sample of each county in the state in 1860 also will be
presented in Chapter 3. A sample of about 400 males 20 and over was
the target size aimed for in each of the 57 counties other than Milwaukee. An attempt was made to sample all of the top 5 to 10 per
cent of returns by examining all returns above $2,000. This proved to
be too time consuming and the level was raised to $5,000 for many
counties.

A very rough guide of the magnitude of random sampling errors for
the sample mean, $\overline{X}$, and Gini coefficient, R, may be established by
assuming a Pareto distribution with a straight line. It will be shown
later in this chapter that this curve is appropriate for the top 50 to 70
per cent of recipients. Its extension to low income or wealth recipients
yields an implicit overall mean not usually more than 20 per cent higher
than the actual mean.

One can generate wealth values of the continuous Pareto curve for
given R. For a Pareto curve of ten points with R of approximately 0.5,
the values are 1.000, 0.250, 0.179, 0.143, 0.121, 0.106, 0.095, 0.086,
0.079, 0.073. These stem from formulas developed by the author[5]
where the top value is arbitrarily set at 1, the second at $(1-R)/(1+2R)$,
and the third to tenth using successive products with factors of $(2+R)/$
$(2+3R)$, $(3+2R)/(3+4R)$, ... $(9+8R)/(9+10R)$. From these values one
may compute $s_{\overline{X}}/\mu$, or the ratio of the standard error of the mean to the
population mean and s_R, or the standard error of the Gini coefficient.[6]
For our ten values, $s_{\overline{X}}/\mu$ is 0.392 and s_R is 0.095. Other possibilities
are:

Sample size, n	$R = 0.200$		$R = 0.500$		$R = 0.800$	
	$s_{\overline{X}}/\mu$	s_R	$s_{\overline{X}}/\mu$	s_R	$s_{\overline{X}}/\mu$	s_R
10	0.133	0.058	0.392	0.095	0.712	0.027
20	.094	.041	.277	.067	.503	.019
40	.067	.029	.196	.047	.356	.013
100	.042	.018	.124	.030	.225	.008
200	.030	.013	.088	.021	.159	.006
400	.021	.009	.062	.015	.112	.004
1,000	.013	.006	.039	.009	.071	.003
2,000	.009	.004	.028	.007	.050	.002

The above calculations have been made assuming the population size
was infinite. The standard errors must be reduced to the extent that
there is 100 per cent sampling in the upper tail of the distribution.

5. *Choice of Microcomponent*

Women were not considered because so very few reported wealth,
and most of those who did were widows. To have included women
would have meant that perhaps more than 95 per cent would have been
in the zero class. The gainfully employed were not selected as the
population to sample because to do so would be to leave out many
young men with no occupation, and to include some as young as 15
years old having an occupation. An age analysis demands that all in
the age class be considered.

The family was not chosen as the microcomponent because of the
large element of unrelated individuals, particularly the young foreign
born. It did not seem reasonable to include a 21-year-old Irish boy
with no wealth and exclude a 21-year-old American-born boy living at
home with $200 wealth. One small sample using the family as the
microcomponent was conducted; it proved to be not very revealing.

Why choose 20 as the cutoff age when many were in the labor force
much earlier in life? The author did, at first, sample the age group
from 15 to 19 but found there was never any case of wealth recorded.
Perhaps this occurred in part because one usually could not buy land
until he was 21. It is true that there was ambiguity about "squatting"
of a minor prior to the government land sale. Age 20 was used because
census population tables were given by sex, with one class having
bounds of 20 and 29. The next lowest class had limits from 15 to 19.

6. *Illegibility*

One disheartening aspect of the sampling procedure was that the
inked writing on some pages had either faded or was sufficiently poor
to begin with that it was impossible to read. This was especially true

when one considers that most samples were taken from microfilm. The only procedure that could be employed with illegible pages was to skip them completely. This occurred on at least 1 per cent of the pages sampled. In some counties it occurred from 5 to 10 per cent of the time.

This meant that the number of males in a county, multiplied by the proper sampling weight, was often less than the actual number reported for the county in published census tables. In some cases it was larger because of random sampling error. The VEOI averages and concentration coefficients for each county are thus representative, technically, only of legible pages. VEOI aggregates obtained from sampling can be compared to VEOI published aggregates only by comparing averages or by boosting the sampling total by a correction factor.

7. *Consistency with National Estimates*

The VEOI, aggregated from Schedule 1, have been published for the United States:

	VEOI aggregate	Male population 20 & up	VEOI males 20 & up
Milwaukee	$ 38,712,145	15,889	$2,434
Wisconsin	294,901,573	199,476	1,478
United States	19,089,156,289	7,970,000	2,395
United States, not including the value of slaves[7]	17,100,000,000	7,970,000	2,140
24 non-slave states and territories	10,370,356,000	5,072,592	2,044

	Value of real estate	Value of personal estate	Value of real estate/VEOI aggregate
Milwaukee	$ 30,285,895	$ 8,426,250	0.783
Wisconsin	233,784,394	71,117,179	.758
United States	10,930,420,259	8,158,736,030	.571
United States, not including the value of slaves	10,900,000,000	6,200,000,000	.637
24 non-slave states and territories	7,146,812,000	3,223,557,291	.689

We see that the Milwaukee average was about the same as that for the

United States and above the average for non-slave states. It was perhaps 10 per cent larger than the United States average with slave
values eliminated.

Are these estimates consistent with national wealth estimates that
have been made for the United States by modern scholars? We examine
the available data, as presented in Table 1. The estimates for the nineteenth century do not include the market value of land and are not available for the specific year 1860. We need a land value estimate and an
interpolated value for reproducible tangible assets. One may examine
the ratio of land value and reproducible tangible assets (in structures,
equipment, inventories, and monetary gold and silver) in an attempt to
see what the implications of trend are for the period from 1850 to 1880.
This is shown in the top time series chart of Exhibit 2. The extrapolated values for 1850, 1860, and 1870 are 0.886, 0.820, and 0.754.
Using reproducible tangible asset values in 1929 prices of $10.8 billion
in 1850 and $53.7 billion in 1880, one can obtain values of $18.4 billion and $31.5 billion in 1860 and 1870 using the compound interest
rate formula or exponential trend. If these are adjusted by the consumer price index of Appendix 3, and combined with our land-asset
value ratios, an estimate of national wealth can be made. Thus, national wealth in 1860 in current (1860) prices might be $18.4 \times 10^9 \times
100/194 \times (1 + 0.820) = $17.3 billion. It might be $31.5 \times 10^9 \times 141/
194 \times (1 + 0.754) = $40.1 billion in 1870 in current prices. For 1850 it
would be the reproducible tangible asset value in current dollars times
the land-asset ratio, or $4.5 \times 10^9 \times (1 + 0.886) = $8.5 billion. We see
at once that our estimate for 1860 of $17.3 billion is very close to the
$17.1 billion of reported VEOI net of slave value. Thus the data for
Milwaukee take on added significance. We can say that they were
similar or slightly larger than the national average in 1860 and that
they are consistent with national wealth estimates of the twentieth century.

There still can be a strong feeling of doubt because of the possible
duplication of asset values. The Milwaukee balance sheet could be
the sum of the balance sheets of many persons where creditor-debtor,
or owner-issuer relationships *among persons* had not been cancelled
or eliminated. One can get some glimpse of the magnitude of this factor by examining the middle portion of Table 1 and the middle chart of
Exhibit 2. In 1955, total asset values of $3,074 \times 10^9 included an
amount for intangible assets encompassing currency, deposits in com-
mercial banks, life insurance reserves, pension and retirement funds,
receivables, loans on securities, mortgages, securities, and equity in
unincorporated business. Total assets, the sum of tangible and intangible assets, were subject to liabilities in categories, leaving an equity
of only $1,809 \times 10^9. Thus, duplication may be measured by the ratio
of $3,074/$1,809 = 1.70, or assets to equity in 1955.

The extent of this duplication, or financial obligations outstanding,
has increased as our economy has grown. The least-squares trend

Table 1. Elements of National Wealth in the United States, 1850—1956

| Year | National wealth in billions of current dollars | | | |
	Total	Reproducible tangible assets (RTA)	Land	Land/RTA
1956	1,448.2	1,199.6	230.8	0.192
1949	900.2	728.7	157.7	0.216
1945	561.2	446.1	117.4	0.263
1939	395.6	305.3	88.6	0.290
1933	330.2	241.0	81.1	0.336
1929	439.1	313.2	113.5	0.362
1922	334.2	233.2	92.8	0.397
1912	165.2	109.1	58.2	0.533
1900	87.7	59.1	30.9	0.522
1900		63.8		
1890		46.1		
1880		25.8		
1850		4.5		

Source: U.S. Bureau of the Census, *Historical Statistics of the United States, Colonial Times to 1957* (GPO: Washington, D.C., 1960), p. 151, Series 197, 198, 215, of National Wealth by Type of Asset, from Raymond W. Goldsmith.

| Year | National Balance Sheet in billions of current dollars | | | | | |
	Total assets	Tangible assets	Intangible assets	Liabilities	Equity	Total Assets/ Equity
1955	3,074.0	1,329.0	1,745.0	1,265.0	1,809.0	1.70
1949	2,016.0	881.3	1,134.7	874.0	1,142.0	1.77
1945	1,557.5	570.3	987.2	772.5	784.9	1.98
1939	877.2	395.0	482.2	356.5	520.6	1.68
1933	733.1	322.4	410.7	281.4	451.7	1.62
1929	981.6	426.9	554.8	324.3	657.4	1.49
1922	653.0	326.2	326.8	222.4	430.6	1.52
1912	308.6	167.6	141.0	94.1	214.5	1.44
1900	159.0	90.2	68.8	47.2	111.9	1.42

Source: *Ibid.*, p. 150, Series 158, 159, 160, 181, 196.

| Year | Value of Stock of structures and equipment in billions of current dollars | | | | | |
	Total of four specified sectors	Agriculture	Mining	Manufac- turing	Transpor- tation & other public utilities	Agriculture/ Total of four
1948	103.9	18.5	5.3	34.8	45.3	0.178
1940	85.2	13.5	4.7	25.3	41.6	0.158
1930	92.9	15.5	6.2	27.0	44.2	0.167
1922	78.0	15.3	5.3	22.0	35.4	0.196
1912	65.1	13.4	3.4	15.3	33.0	0.206
1900	38.5 (39)	8.8	1.6	7.2 (7.6)	21.0	0.229
1890	29.1	7.3	0.8	4.5	16.5	0.251
1880	20.6	6.6	0.4	1.9	11.8	0.320

Source: *Ibid.*, p. 152, Series 247, 248, 249, 250, 251.

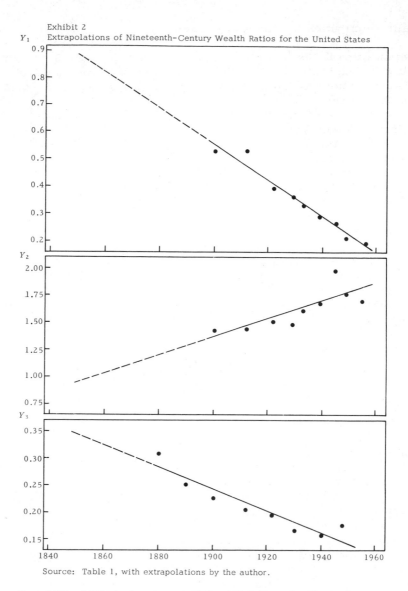

Exhibit 2

Y_1 Extrapolations of Nineteenth-Century Wealth Ratios for the United States

Source: Table 1, with extrapolations by the author.

$Y_{1,t} = 0.886 - 0.0066\,t$, where $t = \text{year} - 1850$ and Y_1 is the ratio of land value to reproducible tangible assets in the United States. Y_1 is series 215 divided by 198.

$Y_{2,t} = 0.959 + 0.0082\,t$, where $t = \text{year} - 1850$ and Y_2 is the ratio of total assets to equity (total assets minus total liabilities) in the United States. Y_2 is series 196 divided by 159.

$Y_{3,t} = 0.345 - 0.002\,t$, where $t = \text{year} - 1850$ and Y_3 is the ratio of the value of stock of structures and equipment in agriculture to the value of stock of structures and equipment in agriculture, mining, and manufacturing and transportation in the United States. Y_3 is series 248 divided by 247.

equation fitted to the Goldsmith ratios of assets to equity is given in Exhibit 2. The implications of the backward extrapolation are that little duplication existed in the middle of the last century. It would seem that we need not worry too much about magnification. It should also be remembered that the VEOI data are presumably the asset values obtained by asking persons what their valuations were. Corporations as such are not included.

It is not impossible to make some crude estimates of the national data which would correspond to the real estate, personal estate dichotomy of our VEOI data. Some estimates by Professor Kuznets on the stock of structures and equipment are presented in the bottom panels of Table 1 and Exhibit 2. The data for the four sectors (agriculture, mining, manufacturing, and transportation and equipment) represented about 80 per cent of the total of stock and equipment in 1880.[8] The least-squares trend extrapolation of agriculture percentages (including the value of farm residences) gives an estimate of 33 in 1860 if one uses the data from 1880 to 1948. The experience in 1880, 1890, and 1900 would indicate a value of 35 to 40 per cent instead of 33 per cent. In any case, 33 per cent may be combined with our earlier land-reproducible tangible asset ratio of 0.820/1. If roughly a third of reproducible tangible assets is agricultural structures, then:

$$\frac{0.820 + (1/3)\,(1)}{1 - (1/3)\,(1)} = \frac{1.15}{0.67} = \frac{1.73}{1}.$$

Thus land value plus value of agricultural structures and equipment are about 63 per cent of total 1860 wealth. It is admitted that this is a rough figure to compare to our VEOI data. It might be better to exclude some farm equipment and include some non-farm residential construction. An alternative is to use Raymond W. Goldsmith's data,[9] noting that in 1850 residential non-farm and farm structures represented 48 per cent of reproducible tangible assets and in 1880 represented 31 per cent. An interpolated value for 1860 would be 37 per cent.

The above 63 and 37 per cent values from the Simon Kuznets and Goldsmith data may be compared to the Schedule 1 results:

	Milwaukee	Wisconsin	United States
VEOI real estate	0.78	0.76	0.64
VEOI personal estate	0.22	0.24	0.36
	1.00	1.00	1.00

The similarity of the two sets of figures for the United States for 1860 suggests again the adequacy of VEOI data. Because the 0.78 and 0.76 ratios of real to personal estate for Milwaukee and Wisconsin are larger than the 0.64 value for the country as a whole, it can be stated that Milwaukee and Wisconsin data have a greater relative weight attached to real estate than to personal estate. This may be a very real

difference, since Wisconsin was so newly developed at that time. The
United States ratio in 1860 of 0.64 from our data is consistent with the
1 - 0.35 to 1 - 0.37 estimates of twentieth-century data.

Richard A. Easterlin has made estimates of income for each of the
various states in 1840 and 1880.[10] For Wisconsin these data are, in
current dollars:

	Total income	Total labor force	Total income per worker
1840	$ 2,000,000	10,000	$239
1880	124,000,000	322,000	384

If one could make 1860 estimates of income from data like these, it
would be interesting to correlate them with 1860 wealth data. The
simple average of the $239 and $384 figures after first adjusting each
to 1860 prices is $296. This is plotted, considering the Wisconsin
VEOI value given earlier of $1,478, as a point in Exhibit 3. The point
is somewhat out of line due to the extremely high 1840 Wisconsin income value of $239, larger than that of any other eastern or northern
central state. The top part of Exhibit 3 considers only 1880 income.
In this case Wisconsin is much more nearly in line. Only California
data do not fit the scheme. The coefficients in the lower diagram are
especially interesting; they imply that at very low levels of wealth, income and wealth are equivalent. If the regression coefficient of 0.77
in $Y = 0.90W^{0.77}$, as defined in the exhibit, could be interpreted as an
exact mathematical value, then income distribution will have considerably less inequality than wealth distribution. Our purpose at this point,
however, is to illustrate that the wealth data are reasonable. One notes
that Wisconsin is in the group of states of early settlement with a relatively high income/wealth ratio.

It is possible to have, on the whole, great confidence in the 1860
census data that are used in this book.

B. WEALTH SIZE AND INEQUALITY AMONG MALES
IN MILWAUKEE IN 1860

The distribution of wealth for 1860 is presented in Table 2 in 1860
dollars. Wealth is defined as VEOI, or the value of real estate and personal estate. The size of both the average wealth and relative dispersion or inequality is startling. The average wealth of $2,376 is the
equivalent of $7,960 when stated in 1960 dollars, using a price index
of 329 (1860 = 100). This is an amount which is still far greater than
average income in 1960.

The inequality level of 0.89 was so large that it was more than 2.5
times the income inequality level in the county in 1959. It will be noted
that the top 0.10 per cent of wealth-holders, or 16 men, had 14 per cent

Exhibit 3
Wealth per Adult Male in 1860, Related to Income per Worker in 1880 and
Income Average per Worker in 1840 and 1880 for Non-Slave States

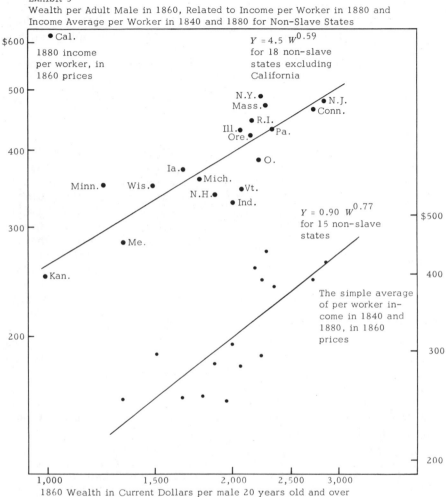

Sources: U.S. Census Office. 8th Census, 1860. *Population of the United States in*
1860 (GPO: Washington, D.C., 1864), pp. 594—99; U.S. Census Office. 8th Census,
1860. *Statistics of the United States (Including Mortality, Property &c.,) in 1860*
(GPO: Washington, 1866), p. 319; Richard A. Easterlin, "Interregional Differences in
Per Capita Income, Population, and Total Income, 1840—1950," in National Bureau of
Economic Research, *Studies in Income and Wealth*, Vol. 24 (Princeton, N.J., 1960), 97—
101. Variant A of 1840 income was used.

Table 2. Distribution of Wealth Among Males 20 Years Old and Over,[a] Milwaukee County, 1860.

Lower limit of wealth class in dollars X	Total number of males in the wealth class	Total amount of wealth in thousands of dollars in the wealth class	N_X or the per cent of total males above the lower limit, X	A_X or the per cent of total wealth above the lower limit, X	Total number of native-born males in wealth class	Total number of foreign-born males in wealth class
			All groups		**Nativity groups**	
0—	5,160	—	100.00	100.00	1,160	4,000
10—	40	—	66.37	100.00	—	40
20—	480	13	66.11	100.00	40	440
50—	800	41	62.98	99.96	40	760
100—	1,520	167	57.76	99.85	160	1,360
200—	1,660	474	47.86	99.39	220	1,440
500—	1,860	1,168	37.04	98.09	240	1,620
1,000—	1,440	1,914	24.91	94.89	180	1,260
2,000—	1,060	3,310	15.53	89.20	200	860
5,000—	680	4,472	8.62	80.56	240	440
10,000—	300	3,857	4.18	68.30	100	200
20,000—	201	5,591	2.23	57.72	130	71
50,000—	95	6,125	0.92	42.39	64	31
100,000—	28	3,669	0.30	25.59	23	5
200,000—	15	3,818	0.12	15.53	14	1
500,000—	3	1,845	0.02	5.06	2	1
	15,342	36,463[b]			2,813	12,529
Arithmetic mean	$2,376				$7,101	$1,302
Median	$ 100				$ 200	$ 100
Gini coefficient	0.893				0.883	0.860

[a] Data were obtained from a sample of 1 of every 20 males 20 years and older whose estates were under $20,000. A complete enumeration was made of estates over $20,000. The $2,376 and 15,342 men obtained from the sample differ from the $2,434 and 15,889 men obtained from 100 per cent addition by census compilers for several reasons: some wealth of women is included in the $2,434 value but not in the $2,376 value; some pages of the schedule were illegible; a few more persons might have been added to the sample if data on age, occupation, and nativity had not been gathered; census additions of VEOI may be subject to some little error; there may be some sampling error. If the twentieth man in the sample had a wealth of $2,000 or more, he was not included in the sample of 1 in 20 in the lower stratum. The per cent of men in the lower stratum of the sample was 97.8 using

$$\sigma_p = \sqrt{1 - \frac{n}{N}} \sqrt{\frac{p(1-p)}{n}}, \text{ we obtain } \sqrt{1 - \frac{750}{15,000}} \sqrt{\frac{0.978 \ (0.022)}{750}} = 0.0052.$$

A 1 per cent random sampling error from a population of 15,000 could account for 150 men.

[b] Figures in this column do not add to total because of rounding.

Source: Schedule 1 of the 1860 Census for Wisconsin.

of the wealth of the 15,342 men in Milwaukee. The top 1 per cent had 44 per cent, and the top 10 per cent held 83 per cent of wealth. The richest 218 men had as much wealth as the poorest 15,142. A statistician might never again witness such an extreme case of skewness, in which the arithmetic mean was 23.8 times the median. It is the purpose of this chapter to unfold some of the mysteries of these measures of central tendency and dispersion so that one might better understand the dynamic situation.

It is of advantage to relate the average wealth of $2,376 to average income in 1860. In Milwaukee County in 1860, average annual wages in manufacturing were $264; carpenter rates were $250 to $320; day labor rates were from $150 to $250. It will be shown in the income supplement that 1864 income distribution with the Pareto extension had an average income of $414, expressed in 1864 dollars, or $264, when expressed in 1860 dollars. Let us use $250 as the income average for males in 1860. A wealth-income ratio of $2,376/$250 or 9.5 in 1860 would seem to be extremely large. The richest man could buy the labor of nearly 3,000 average-income persons in that year. The wealth held by the top 18 persons was sufficient in magnitude to equal the wages of the 15,324 men in the county for the year. There was thus extreme inequality in potential power.

It is instructive to examine in detail the characteristics of the rich people of the county. This may be done with the list of the top 46 men, arrayed by total wealth, shown in Table 3. These rich were largely native born, exactly half of them having been born in New York. The foreign born, being 80 per cent of the adult male population of the county, are represented in this list by only 8 individuals, or 17 per cent of the 46 men. The median age of the group is 44 years, considerably higher than the median of 35 for all men 20 and older. The average size of the families, including servants, was 7.7; the average number of servants per family was 2.5.

These 46 rich men each held more than $100,000 in wealth, which would be $1,000,000 by today's standards if one considers that prices in 1960 were 3.33 times those of 1860 and that productivity would lead to a similar factor if real wealth per capita increased at a moderate rate of 1.2 per cent a year. The 46 constituted over half of the 86 men above $100,000 in the state as a whole. Of the 11 richest men in the state, 8 lived in Milwaukee. This is a rather large number of "1960 millionaires" in so newly developed an area.[11]

The list of 46 is headed by Mr. Alexander Mitchell, banker and railroad developer; he was to emerge in the decade of the 1860's as a prominent tycoon. The second-, third-, and fifth-ranked individuals were listed as real estate dealers. They held large amounts of land in the city, having come early to the county: Elisha Eldred, the second-ranked man, came to Milwaukee in 1842, fifth-ranked Byron Kilbourn in 1835. The latter purchased 129 acres of land in southeast Milwaukee in that year at $1.25 an acre. His father, a congressman, had been prom-

Table 3. Data on the 46 Males Having Wealth of More than $100,000, Milwaukee County, 1860

Name[a]	Age	Occupation	Real estate	Personal estate	Place of birth	Family size
Alexander Mitchell	41	banker	$400,000	$300,000	Scotland	7(2)[b]
Elisha Eldred	64	real estate	500,000	100,000	New York	10(5)
James H. Rogers	65	real estate	500,000	45,000	New York	9(4)
James B. Martin	45	banker	350,000	10,000	Maryland	10(5)
Byron Kilbourn	58	real estate	300,000	2,000	Connecticut	9(3)
Daniel Newhall	39	merchant	300,000	2,000	Mass.	10(2)
Lemuel W. Weeks	54	pres., ins. co.	300,000	2,000	Vermont	7(3)
James Ludington	33	banker	250,000	50,000	New York	4
James Kneeland	42	farmer, real est.	270,000	11,000	New York	5(3)
John M. Henni	52	R.C. Bishop	250,000	2,000	Switzerland	7(3)
Charles T. Bradley	42	merchant	250,000	1,500	Mass.	5(3)
William H. Metcalf	38	merchant	250,000	1,500	New York	7(3)
George D. Dousman	42	merchant	200,000	25,000	Michigan	11(3)
John J. Orton	43	attorney	210,000	5,000	New York	1
Hans Crocker	41	real est. owner	150,000	50,000	New York	4(?)
William P. Lynde	46	lawyer	100,000	100,000	New York	13(5)
John H. Medbury	53	banker	150,000	50,000	New York	6(2)
Martin B. Medbury	55	miller	150,000	50,000	New York	7(3)
John H. Tweedy	45	lawyer	150,000	40,000	Connecticut	8(3)
Harrison Ludington	47	lumber mer.	150,000	15,000	New York	12(3)
Daniel Wells, Jr.	51	lumber manu.	150,000	15,000	Maine	8(2)
J. L. Pierce	60	merchant	156,500	5,000	New Hamp.	7(1)
James R. Cross	40	banker	150,000	10,000	New York	5(3)
Moses Kneeland	52	real estate[c]	150,000	10,000	New York	9(3)
John C. Starkweather	29	lawyer	113,530	41,169	New York	8(4)
James S. Brown	36	lawyer	150,000	2,000	Maine	7(3)
John L. McVickar	30	lumber dealer	100,000	50,000	New York	4(2)
Harry Birchard	59	real estate	120,000	25,000	Connecticut	5(2)
Levi J. Mesnitt	52	lawyer	130,000	13,000	Maine	11(1)
Walter P. Flanders	53	lawyer	135,000	6,000	New Hamp.	7(1)
Jacob Mahler	38	merchant	60,000	75,000	Germany	3(1)
Joshua Hathaway	49	real estate	100,000	30,000	New York	11(2)
George H. Walker	48	miller	100,000	25,000	Virginia	7(3)
Albert B. Van Cott	49	jeweller	90,000	35,000	New York	9(1)
John Furlong	47	merchant	100,000	20,000	Ireland	14(4)
Ephraim Mariner	33	lawyer	110,000	9,000	New York	9(1)
Charles E. Wendt	33	distiller	100,000	15,000	Brunswick	10(3)
Alonzo L. Kane	37	hotel keeper	100,000	5,000	New York	8(?)
John H. Silkman	43	real estate	100,000	5,000	New York	4(?)
Cicero Comstock	43	banker[c]	100,000	3,000	Ohio	8(1)
Charles Quentin	49	real estate	100,000	2,500	Prussia	9(2)
Otis H. Waldo	38	lawyer	100,000	2,000	New York	11(4)
William Diedrick	58	(no title)	100,000	1,000	Prussia	8(3)
William S. Amos	42	lumber mer.	70,000	30,000	Scotland	8(3)
William S. Candee	26	dry goods mer.	25,000	75,000	New York	8(1)
Samuel L. Rose	43	lawyer	65,000	35,000	New York	4(2)

[a]Names have been verified as much as possible in Starr and Sons, *Directory of the City of Milwaukee*, 1859–1860, and 1860–1861.

[b]Family size includes servants; the number of servants is given in parenthesis. Question mark indicates a lack of clarity in the schedule.

[c]This person was also described as "Gentleman."

Source: Schedule 1 of the 1860 Census.

inent in deciding land settlement policies in the Northwest Territory.[12]
Of the 46 men, 9 were in real estate, 10 were lawyers, 6 were bankers,
and 10 were merchants; only 1 indicated that he was a manufacturer.
Their residential pattern in Milwaukee was a series of clusters: 24 of
the men lived in Ward 7, 10 in Ward 4, 9 in Ward 1, and 1 each in
Wards 3, 6, and 9.

One is led to believe that corporate activity in Milwaukee in 1860
did not involve a large share of total wealth. The 1860 census report
lists only $2,990,000 as the amount of capital invested in 558 manu-
facturing establishments. A compendium listing of these 558 is given
in Table 4. The indication is that almost all of the companies were
small, since the averages are only 5.6 employees and $5,360 in invest-
ment per establishment. The total investment is less than $3 million
of the $36 million holdings reported in Table 2. This is certainly an
indication that these enterprises could have been in the non-corporate
sector. The number of incorporations in Milwaukee by 1860, excluding
religious organizations, was only a handful. It is true that by 1860,
however, railroads had made an impact: data available only for the
state show that from 1850 to 1860, track mileage increased from 20 to
922 and costs of construction increased from $600,000 to $34,000,000.[13]
This latter sum was over 10 per cent of wealth in Wisconsin in 1860.
How much of the cost might be allocated to Milwaukee County and how
much of Milwaukee's share might be accounted for in our wealth data
are difficult questions to answer. Apparently, Milwaukee's was an
economic system only on the verge of modern industrialism. Real estate holdings played a dominant role in an economy of agriculture and
small industry.

Table 4. Ten Manufacturing Industries Employing the Most Capital,
          Milwaukee County, 1860

Field	Number of establishments	Total capital invested	Total number of male employees
Gas	2	$ 396,150	36
Flour and meal	19	383,000	96
Liquors, malt	26	356,000	112
Men's clothing	27	173,900	374
Provisions, pork and beef	8	155,000	60
Boots and shoes	50	145,695	298
Leather	9	141,500	95
Machinery, steam engines	9	134,500	114
Liquors, distilled	15	124,650	42
Soap and candles	9	83,925	30
Other industries	384	895,850	1,853
Totals	*558*	*$2,990,170*	*3,110*

Source: U.S. Census Office. 8th Census, 1860. *Statistics of the United States (Including Mortality, Property, &c.,) in 1860* (GPO: Washington, D.C., 1866), pp.648, 649.

Milwaukee County began with nothing but virgin soil in 1835. By 1860, average real estate holdings were 0.783 ($2,376), or $1,760. Assuming a man had arrived in 1835 with the low median wealth of $100 (the median wealth in Milwaukee in 1860), he would have experienced a growth of wealth of the magnitude $1,760 = 100 (1 + r)^{25}$. In this case $(1 + r) = 1.084$. There was magic in an 8 per cent rate of growth per annum, and we are about to encounter this figure again.

C. AGE AND NATIVITY OF MILWAUKEE WEALTHHOLDERS

We have seen that there was extreme inequality of wealth distribution. The concentration coefficient of the logarithms of wealth was 0.44, with a mean difference in logarithms to the base 10 of 1.82 where those with zero wealth were given value of $W = \$1$. This means that the average ratio of one man's wealth to that of another was 66 in Milwaukee. If one person could meet another in Milwaukee on some random basis, not cloistered by ward, the mathematical expectation is that one of the two men would have wealth 66 times that of the other.

In spite of this inequality, the literature in the 1850's and 1860's stressed the free play that one had for his talents, and the reward one would obtain for his abilities and efforts. Freeman Hunt, in his *Worth and Wealth, a Collection of Maxims, Morals, and Miscellanies for Merchants and Men of Business* stated the rules for the accumulation of wealth:

In the first place, make up your mind to accomplish whatever you undertake; decide upon some particular employment and persevere in it. All difficulties are overcome by diligence and assiduity. Do not be afraid to work with your own hands, and diligently, too. "A cat in gloves catches no mice." Attend to your own business and never trust it to another. "A pot that belongs to many is ill sturred and worse boiled." Be frugal. "That which will not make a pot will make a pot lid." Be abstemious. "Who dainties love shall beggars prove." Rise early. "The sleeping fox catches no poultry." Treat every one with respect and civility. "Everything is gained and nothing lost by courtesy." Good manners insure success. Never anticipate wealth from any other source than labor. "He who waits for dead men's shoes may have to go for a long time barefoot." And above all things, "NIL DESPERANDUM," for "Heaven helps those who help themselves." If you implicitly follow these precepts, nothing can hinder you from accumulating.[14]

One wonders how this optimism could prevail if so few held so much wealth. The problem, then, is one of solving the apparent conflict between the fact of extreme economic inequality and the belief that individual effort would produce economic growth. The data must be examined from the standpoint of the age of the individual, and his background studied to gain understanding. By all measures, the best proxy for measuring the abilities, feelings, and accumulative ingenuity of the individual in the period is whether the individual was born in the United States or immigrated from a foreign country.

Exhibit 4
Number of Native-Born and Foreign-Born Males Classified by Age
for Milwaukee County in 1860[a]

Number of males in
one-year interval

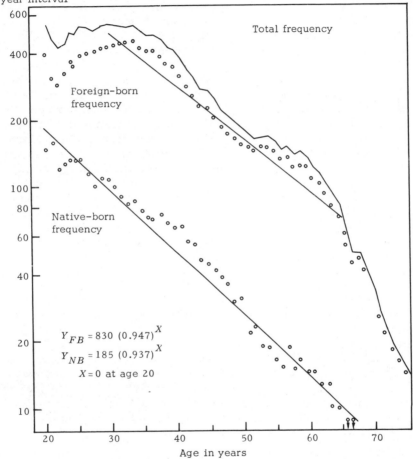

$$Y_{FB} = 830 \, (0.947)^X$$
$$Y_{NB} = 185 \, (0.937)^X$$
$$X = 0 \text{ at age } 20$$

Age in years

[a]Data for ages 26 to 66 are 10-year moving averages. Lesser periods have
been used in smoothing the data outside this range. The least-squares regression
equation for foreign born was fitted to 35 frequencies between ages 30 and 65.
The equation for native born was fitted to 46 moving average values between ages
20 and 65.

Source: Sample from Schedule 1 of the 1860 Census.

Exhibit 4 shows graphically the number of native-born and foreign-born males, by age group, in Milwaukee. The pattern is sufficiently clear-cut that some generalizations can be made. The first least-squares equation is $Y_{NB} = 185 \ (0.937)^X$, $20 \leq$ age ≤ 65. Y_{NB} is the number of native-born males in Milwaukee and $X =$ age $- 20$. The number of males of a particular age is thus, on the average, 6.3 per cent less than the number one year younger. The configuration for foreign born in 1860 is clear between ages 30 and 65. There is a noticeable drop in the frequency pattern for ages under 30 and over 65. In the pattern range, $Y_{FB} = 830 \ (0.947)^X$, $30 \leq$ age ≤ 65, so that frequencies decrease 5.3 per cent in going from one age group to the next-older group.

The 0.937 and 0.947, or their respective complements of 6.3 per cent and 5.3 per cent, would exactly reflect population growth if there were a closed society with no deaths and no mobility except for foreign immigrants, all arriving each year at age 30. Milwaukee's adult male population actually grew at an annual average rate of 6.6 per cent from 1850 to 1860. It is certainly no coincidence that this figure is only slightly larger than our 1860 frequency-age coefficients, particularly the 6.3 per cent figure for native-born persons.

There is another relationship in Exhibit 4 which will be employed to great advantage. It is noted that the number of foreign born is approximately four times as large as that for native born for a given age interval. It is further noted that the number of native born in a given one-year age interval, X, is equivalent to the number in the foreign born one-year age interval, $X + 30$. Since 30 years may be thought of as one generation, the data can be thought of as encompassing two generations. The foreign born come into the labor force at a 6 per cent annual rate. After 30 years their 20-year old native-born sons appear in the labor force. If this model were correct, analysis of a point in time would yield the diagram we have.

We now turn to the most interesting configuration of all, Exhibit 5. The average wealth for age-nativity groups vividly quantifies the reality of America's dream of material progress. The native-born wealth average increases rapidly from age 20 to age 43, increases very little from age 45 to 60, and then is very substantial for the few men above 65. Can we not generalize this pattern with a simple exponential-trend growth model? It is:

$$W_{NB,X} = \$1,310 \ (1.083)^X, \text{ where } W_{NB} \text{ is wealth and } X = \text{age} - 20.$$

The first answer to our slope coefficient is that the growth rate in the wealth of an individual was 8.3 per cent a year. The problem is that the individuals of age X are not the same individuals as those of age $X + 1$. Really to know the wealth growth rate from age 20 to 70 would necessitate studying the wealth of an age cohort from 1810 to 1860.

Exhibit 5

Average Wealth of Native-Born and Foreign-Born Males Classified by Age for Milwaukee County in 1860[a]

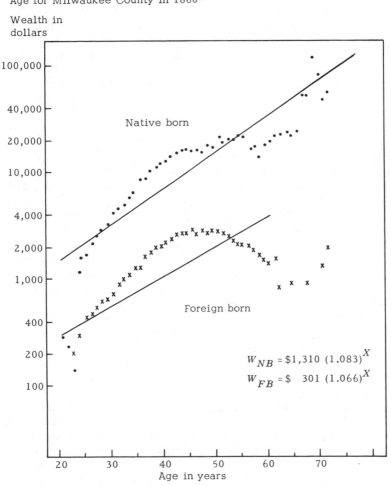

Wealth in
dollars

Native born

Foreign born

$$W_{NB} = \$1,310\ (1.083)^X$$
$$W_{FB} = \$\ \ 301\ (1.066)^X$$

Age in years

[a]Data for ages 26 to 66 are 10-year moving averages. Lesser periods have been used in smoothing the data outside this range. The least-squares regression equation for native born was fitted to 52 averages from ages 21 to 72, and the equation for foreign born was fitted to 41 points from ages 20 to 60.

Source: Sample from Schedule 1 of the 1860 Census.

The relationship in Exhibit 4 is for 1860. If average real wealth increased 2 per cent from 1860 to 1861, the line for that year might run
parallel to but 2 per cent higher than the line in 1860. The individual
who remained alive might have then experience a (1.083)(1.02), or a
10.4 per cent increase in wealth.

In fact, it is obviously true that one can easily visualize a model
with no increase in the overall average wealth from one year to the
next which still has great age incentive. One merely starts with little
at age 20, say $1,000. He accumulates at a rate of 8.3 per cent a year
for 50 years so that when he dies he has $1,000 $(1.083)^{50}$ = $54,000.
His wealth could be distributed among 54 men of age 20. All that is
necessary for this model to continue in perpetuity is that the number of
20-year-olds should be 54 times as large as the number of 70-year-
olds. This could occur if our population of 20-year-olds increased at
a rate of 8.3 per cent a year.

If, however, the population increases only 6.3 per cent a year, while
wealth in real and personal estate is being accumulated at 8.3 per cent,
the wealth of the old man would be sufficient to give $(1.063)^{50}$, or 21
young men with ($54,000/21) = $2,580. Thus these young men start out
50 years after our old man with an amount $1,000 $(1.02)^{50}$ = $2,580.

But our rich old man does not randomly distribute his accumulated
wealth. We have no data on how much wealth sons inherited from their
fathers in 1860. But insight can be obtained by looking at the age-
specific wealth averages for foreign born. The native-born persons in
1860 were largely the sons of foreign-born persons in the preceding
generation. Exhibit 5 shows somewhat the same pattern for foreign-
born as that for native-born persons from age 20 to age 50. It is only
the wealth of the foreign born above age 50 that does not fit the scheme.
Perhaps this older group came late to America with their immigrant children and thus had no opportunity to accumulate wealth in America; perhaps, because of different customs pertaining to the care of elders,
this group had already transferred their wealth to their American-born
sons.[15]

In any case, we may fit a least-squares regression line to the data
from age 20 to age 60, obtaining $W_{FB,X}$ = $301 $(1.066)^{X}$. Here again
we have an apparent accumulation rate of 6.6 per cent a year with a
population growth rate of 5.3 per cent. This leaves a per capita accumulation of 1.3 per cent a year. It is perhaps carrying statistical
manipulations too far to point out that eliminating a few of the points
near age 60 would yield a per capita accumulation of 2 per cent. For
example, the exponential trend fitted to $20 \leq X \leq 55$ gives an apparent
rate of 9.1 per cent a year.

The pattern is that there is a 30-year lag in the average wealth of
foreign-born persons behind that of the native born.

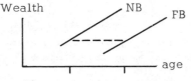

30 years or one generation

If we push our pattern to its extreme, we say that we are capturing the scheme of a foreign-born parent and his son one generation later. It is noted that the age-specific wealth average of a native-born person is approximately 6 times that of the foreign born:

$$Y_{NB}/Y_{FB} = 5.9 \text{ when } X = 40-20.$$

The data for overall averages given in Table 2 was $7,101 for native-born and $1,302 for foreign-born males 20 years old and over, or a ratio of 5.4 to 1. If this ratio is accounted for by a 30-year time span, then $5.9 = 1(1+r)^{30}$, and $1 + r = 1.061$.

It is true that 6.1 per cent is neither the 8.3 per cent apparent rate for native born nor the 6.6 per cent apparent rate for foreign born. There are many possible explanations of why this might be true; ours is that there was no growth rate in Europe from the time the one generation migrated until the next migrated. The following generalization can be made. The 1860 data capture the history of nearly 90 years growth in wealth. This is obtained from the history of foreign-born persons of age 20 to 60 and their sons from age 20 to 70. It is a history of population growth of from 5.3 per cent to 6.3 per cent a year. It is a history of individual wealth accumulation of from 6.2 per cent to 8.3 per cent a year. It is a history of per capita wealth accumulation of from 1 per cent to 2 per cent a year.

The most positive relationship occurs with native-born data, of persons who never left the United States or American territories. Here the per capita growth rate is 2 per cent a year. This coincides with the rate estimates for per capita reproducible tangible assets of Professor Goldsmith, who has estimated that this growth rate averaged 2 per cent per head per annum in the period from 1805 to 1950.[16]

The pattern is not complete unless an explanation is given of what could happen to the wealth of the rich native born. This might be used to establish a staircase for a second generation. Our data are not so large that we can fully establish this model.

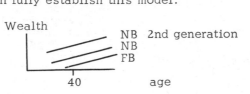

A complete enumeration of 40-year old men was made for the city of

Table 5. Average Total Wealth of 40-Year-Old Males, Classified by
          Country or State of Birth, Milwaukee City, 1860

Place of birth	Number of men	Arithmetic mean	Median
Native born			
New York, Delaware, New Jersey	48	$16,090	$1,850
Maine, Vermont, New Hampshire	12	11,040	2,000
Connecticut, Mass., Rhode Island	21	3,520	1,000
Pennsylvania, Ohio, Ind., Ill., Mich., Wis.	16	4,760	0
Other	24	390	25
All native born	*121*	*8,800*	*450*
Foreign born			
England	22	7,050	600
Ireland	115	1,860	50
Germany	217	1,300	200
Scotland	17	590	0
Holland	14	450	250
Norway, Denmark	8	460	0
Other	54	700	150
All foreign born	*447*	*1,610*	*100*
All 40-year-olds	*568*	*3,200*	*150*

Source: National Archives Microfilm Publications, 1860 Census Population Schedules, Wisconsin, Microfilm copy no. T-7, Roll no. 311.

Milwaukee only. Results are given in Table 5. Among native born, the
New York-, Delaware-, and New Jersey-born wealth average is 3.5
times that of the Pennsylvania-, Ohio-, Indiana-, Michigan-, and Wis-
consin-born average. In part, this is a measure of the difference between the first and the second generation native.

    Among the foreign born, we note the English average is nearly that
of the native-born average. Surprisingly, the Irish average for 40-year-
olds was next in line; there were a few rich Irish men. The Dutch and
Norwegian averages were almost a generation below that of the foreign-
born average. The German level is a generation behind that of the
English. We have, then, a model which is almost a helix, or one side
of a spiral staircase.

    If one were to follow the generations argument literally, he would
expect the 46 rich men of Table 3 to have progenitors born in the United
States. No methodical check has been made, other than to examine
some lists leading to genealogical histories of 2[17] of the 46. In the
case of Byron Kilbourn, the fifth-richest man in 1860, one can trace
the paternal line as follows:

	Year of birth	Place of birth
Byron Kilbourn	1801	Connecticut
James Kilbourn	1770	Connecticut
Josiah Kilbourn	1731	Connecticut
Josiah Kilbourn	1702	Connecticut
Ebenezer Kilbourn	1665	America
John Kilbourn	1624	England
Thomas Kilbourn	1578	England

For Moses Kneeland or his brother, James Kneeland, we have:

	Year of birth	Place of birth
Moses Kneeland	1809	New York
David Kneeland	1772	Connecticut
? Kneeland	1752	Connecticut
Izac Kneeland	1716	Connecticut
Benjamin Kneeland	1679	Connecticut

It is noted that the average number of years between father and son for native born was 34 years for the Kilbourns and 35 years for the Kneelands. In the one case, the first ancestor was born in America in 1665, or 136 years prior to the birth of the Milwaukee resident; in the other case, the first known born in America was in 1679, or 130 years prior. At 8 per cent, $(1.08)^{130} = 22,100$. At 6 per cent, $(1.06)^{130} = 1,940$. Even the latter figure is much too high for interpretation unless one compares the $300,000 of Byron Kilbourn and the $150,000 of Moses Kneeland (or his brother, James Kneeland, at $250,000) with the median for Milwaukee native born and foreign born of $100 to $200. Data to be presented on inheritance in Chapter 7 indicate that if the family has more than two children, there is slippage in the wealth aggregate from one generation to the next.[18] Surely one must not carry the compound interest formula to the extreme or he soon has a sum greater than all the resources in the world.

The nativity hurdle is much more than one of maintaining and augmenting the inheritance of estates of non-human wealth. One inherits a culture from his progenitors and their countries of residence which might be called estates of human wealth. The activities of wealth accumulation are affected strongly by the role of communications, of language, of knowledge of markets. Foreign born had limited access to knowledge of employment and land. They were often cloistered among those speaking their own languages. The barriers of the native born were not so confined. One of the very rich of Milwaukee had a father who worked with land problems as a congressman from Ohio. How did his very young son decide to come to Milwaukee at the time of its settlement? Knowledge of markets was surely wider, on the average, among second- and third-generation Americans.

It will be remembered that we are dealing with the average wealth of an age-specific nativity group. There is large dispersion of individual wealth figures from this average. This within-class dispersion is surely large enough to encompass any shirtsleeves-to-shirtsleeves phenomenon within three generations. To emphasize that our age-nativity classifications account for only a part of total inequality, we present Exhibit 6. The Lorenz curve of Milwaukee wealth is shown with its concentration coefficient of 0.893, stated here as $R(X_{W.W})$, where the variate wealth has been ordered from lowest to highest value. Wealth has been ordered by wealth. Suppose we order wealth data not by wealth but by considering nativity-age ordering. We begin with foreign born, first getting the wealth of 20-year-olds, 21-year-olds, ..., 70-year-olds. Then we consider native-born persons ordered by age. The resulting Lorenz curve is plotted with its concentration coefficient $R(X_{W.FB,A,NB,A}) = 0.537$. If age and nativity had had no relationship to wealth, it would have been expected that the Lorenz curve would be a straight line with an R exactly zero except for some short-run random deviations. We have in fact explained 0.537/0.893, or 60.1 per cent of total inequality by considering age-nativity. The explanation was most unsatisfactory among the oldest foreign-born groups. Assuming perfect equality within the foreign- and native-born groups alone explains 41.5 per cent:

$$R(X_{W.FB,NB})/R(X_{W.W}) = 0.371/0.893 = 41.5 \text{ per cent.}$$

The age-nativity explanation does not account for 40 per cent of inequality of wealth. This amount is easily sufficient to account for the luck, physique, drive, ability, effort, or individual performance in wealth accumulation.

In this chapter, a description of the distribution of wealth for Milwaukee in 1860 has been presented after discussing the scope and limitations of the 1860 Census of Wealth. Milwaukee's distribution was extremely unequal with a Gini R of 0.89. Approximately 50 of the county's 15,000 adult men were very rich, having one-fourth of the wealth. Surprisingly, one could almost duplicate the distribution from a normal distribution $[n(\mu,\sigma) = n\,(1.00, .16)]$ using X^{18}. This suggests the role of individual intelligence quotients and the free play of luck, physique, drive, ability, effort, or individual performance in wealth accumulation to the neglect of group action.

The distribution was examined considering the distributions of age and nativity of the men involved. This study strongly suggested that the wealth accumulation of a man was 6 to 8 per cent a year and that per capita wealth accumulation was 1 to 2 per cent a year. There was also the suggestion that the average wealth of a foreign-born person lagged behind that of a native-born person by 30 years, or one generation, and that the pattern was repeated among first- and second-generation native born.

Exhibit 6
The Lorenz Curve for Wealth among Males 20 Years Old and Over
in Milwaukee in 1860, and That Part Explained by Nativity-Age

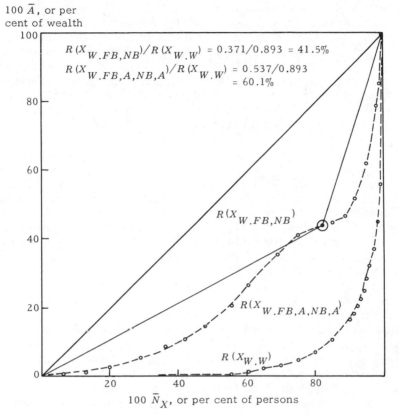

100 $\bar{A}$, or per
cent of wealth

$R(X_{W.FB,NB})/R(X_{W.W}) = 0.371/0.893 = 41.5\%$

$R(X_{W.FB,A,NB,A})/R(X_{W.W}) = 0.537/0.893$
$= 60.1\%$

$R(X_{W.FB,NB})$

$R(X_{W.FB,A,NB,A})$

$R(X_{W.W})$

100 $\bar{N}_X$, or per cent of persons

Source: Sample from Schedule 1 of the 1860 Census.

This means that the individual effort was tempered by the dominating
influence of economic growth. A system of extreme inequality at a
point in time could be tolerated because of the obvious increases in
expected and real wealth values over time. This analysis has been
limited solely to Milwaukee County, but it is true also of other densely
populated areas in 1860. We turn next to a study of Wisconsin as a
whole, where rural influences give a different setting, one of less inequality, one with smaller nativity differentials, but one again of great
economic growth.

Chapter 3

The Distribution of
Wealth in Wisconsin and
Its Counties in 1860

This chapter studies wealth data on two levels, one for the state, the other for counties. The first considers the state as a whole; the microcomponent is the individual, classified by his wealth, age, nativity, and occupation. Two samples were drawn from the state's adult male population of 200,000: one was a non-stratified sample of size 9,542; the other was a much larger sample of 47,931, stratified by wealth and county, in which age, nativity, and occupation were not considered. The stratified sample gave greater detail of high wealth groups, but essentially it was drawn to provide data for the county study.

Because so many data are published by county, including population densities, improved acreage, land inequality, labor rates, and number of persons in manufacturing, it is desirable to study wealth averages and dispersion for each of Wisconsin's counties. One could gain a better understanding of the effect of settlement if one studied the whole range from the 15,900 adult males in Milwaukee County to the 119 in La Pointe (now Bayfield), the 56th county (the 57th and 58th counties had only a few people in each and will not usually be considered). Thus the microcomponent is the county and the number of cases is 56. It is true that the variables were obtained from a study of individuals. However, the published census data are by county, and only the Gini R for each county is calculated from individual data for 1860 since VEOI aggregates are published by county.

A. A NON-STRATIFIED SAMPLE OF WEALTHHOLDINGS
OF INDIVIDUALS IN WISCONSIN

A painstaking sample was taken of approximately each twentieth individual in the census manuscripts for 1860. The sample was de-

signed effectively so each of the 40 lines on a page had an equal
probability of being chosen. The age, nativity (native born or foreign
born), occupation (farmer or non-farmer), and wealth in real plus personal estate were obtained for each male 20 years old or older. Frequency distributions of wealth using these variables are given in
Tables 6, 7, and 8. The 9,542 adult males obtained from the sample
represent only 95 per cent of one-twentieth of adult males in the
state (the 5 per cent error may be attributed in part to the problem
of legibility, discussed at length in Chapter 2). It is assumed that
the 5 per cent of unknown individuals have the same characteristics
as the 95 per cent sampled.

Considerable detail is given in Table 6 in order to show the grati-
fying regularity of the distributions. If one studies the overall dis-

Table 6. Frequency Distributions of Wealth Values for Males 20 and Older,
Classified by Age, Wisconsin, 1860

Dollar value of lower-class limit	Age					
	20 & up	20−29	30−39	40−49	50−59	60−69
	(The ratio of the number of adult males in the cell in 1860 to the number of adult males in Wisconsin in 1860)					
0−	0.288	0.166	0.058	0.025	0.015	0.013
1−	.041	.015	.013	.006	.003	.003
100−	.062	.020	.023	.010	.005	.004
200−	.049	.016	.017	.009	.005	.002
300−	.037	.011	.013	.007	.003	.002
400−	.032	.008	.013	.007	.003	.001
500−	.034	.008	.013	.007	.003	.002
600−	.029	.007	.010	.007	.003	.002
700−	.025	.005	.009	.006	.002	.002
800−	.024	.004	.009	.005	.004	.002
900−	.021	.005	.006	.005	.003	.002
1,000−	.027	.005	.009	.006	.005	.002
1,100−	.019	.003	.008	.006	.002	.001
1,200−	.023	.005	.006	.006	.004	.002
1,300−	.032	.006	.011	.007	.005	.002
1,500−	.058	.010	.019	.017	.007	.003
2,000−	0.46	.006	.016	.013	.008	.004
2,500−	.027	.002	.008	.010	.005	.002
3,000−	.041	.004	.013	.014	.006	.003
4,000−	.023	.002	.007	.007	.005	.002
5,000−	.042	.003	.011	.016	.008	.003
10,000−	.019	.002	.006	.006	.004	.001
	1.000[a]	0.311[a]	0.301[a]	0.199[a]	0.108	0.059[a]
Median	$ 350	$ 0	$ 600	$1,100	$1,050	$ 710
$\bar{X}$	$1,486	$504	$1,506	$2,243	$2,763	$1,718
R	0.752	0.832	0.710	0.654	0.722	0.699

[a]Figures in these columns do not add to totals because of rounding.

Source: Based on a sample of males 20 and older of size 9,542, obtained by examining
one line in each legible 20 of the census manuscripts. The sample accounts for 190,840
of the 199,476 adult males in 1860.

tribution below \$1,200 using classes with intervals of \$100, he sees
that the function decreases continuously to a value of \$100 and to zero
dollars if the zero and \$1—\$99 classes are combined. The two excep-
tions are the classes from \$500—\$599 and \$1,000—\$1,099, since there
was a little tendency to round estimates to \$500 or \$1,000. The distribution thus has essentially the shape of a reverse J with many cases
near or at zero dollars. It is not a Pareto form, however. A Pareto
straight line would have been achieved only if frequencies had continued to unfold below \$1,000 in their reverse J form, with essentially
no wealth values below \$600. Some results from Pareto assumptions
are given in Chapter 6 where comparisons are made with 1963 data.

In Table 6 we encounter the factor of age for the first time. This
factor will be examined extensively, as it was in Chapter 2, because
of its clues about growth trends. We have our familiar pattern of
wealth increase from age 20 to 50 or 55, with a tapering after this age:

Age	$\bar{X}$	R	Age	$\bar{X}$	R
20—24	\$ 283	0.89	50—54	\$2,847	0.73
25—29	727	.77	55—59	2,637	.71
30—34	1,266	.72	60—64	1,643	.67
35—39	1,779	.69	65—69	1,510	.77
40—44	2,109	.66			
45—49	2,450	.65	70 & up	1,296	.79

We also note a decrease in relative dispersion up to age 50 and then
a rise. The pattern for R in relation to age is almost the converse of
that of $\bar{X}$.

Tables 7 and 8 further classify wealth by nativity (NB, FB) and occupation (F, NF). The nativity distinction between native and foreign
born is clear. The farmer—non-farmer distinction is difficult in the
case of farm labor. A person may have been called a laborer while
living in a household whose head stated his occupation as farmer.
Such people were classified as non-farmers unless the occupation was
clearly stated as "farm laborer."[1] It is important to note that the
farmer—non-farmer dichotomy is not exactly a rural-urban dichotomy,
since there were non-farmers living in rural areas. In many ways the
farmer—non-farmer distinction is more germane to wealth distribution
than the rural-urban distinction because farm land ownership plays
such an important role.

Table 7 indicates that 60 per cent of adult males were farmers, as
determined largely by the age group 20—29, consisting of nearly one
third of the cases. This farmer—non-farmer ratio was as large as 2 to
1 for older age groups. In the sample as a whole, 45 per cent of the
adults were native born so this ratio was somewhat independent of
age. The average age for the several groups was $\bar{X}_{all}$ = 37.6, $\bar{X}_{F,NB}$ =
38.2, $\bar{X}_{F,FB}$ = 39.2, $\bar{X}_{NF,NB}$ = 35.9, and $\bar{X}_{NF,FB}$ = 36.2. The table for

means illustrates the now familiar pattern with respect to age for the various classifications. The arithmetic mean for native born was twice that of foreign born. Surprisingly, the mean wealth of non-farmers was 84 per cent of the average for farmers. For those 30 to 50, the non-farmer average was greater than the farmer average. This was also true when these groups were classified by nativity, with but one exception. The relatively high average of native-born farmers between age 50 and 59 is a combination of $\overline{W}_{50-54} = \$5,080$ and $\overline{W}_{55-59} = \$4,041$.

Table 7. Number, Mean, and Concentration Coefficient of Real Estate Values of Males 20 and Older, Classified by Age, Nativity, and Occupation, Wisconsin, 1860

Nativity–Occupation	20 & up	20–29	30–39	40–49	50–59	60–69
(The ratio of the number of adult males in the cell in 1860 to the number of adult males in Wisconsin in 1860)						
All persons	1.000[a]	0.311	0.301	0.199	0.108	0.059
Native born	.450	.152	.127	.087	.049	.025
Foreign born	.550	.159	.174	.112	.059	.034
Farmers	.598	.173	.169	.125	.074	.041
Native born	.279	.089	.075	.055	.035	.018
Foreign born	.319	.084	.094	.070	.039	.023
Non-farmers	.403	.139	.132	.074	.034	.019
Native born	.171	.064	.052	.032	.014	.008
Foreign born	.232	.075	.080	.042	.020	.011
(The arithmetic mean in dollars)						
All persons	1,486	504	1,506	2,243	2,763	1,718
Native born	1,958	629	1,942	2,921	4,180	2,599
Foreign born	1,100	383	1,189	1,772	1,594	1,042
Farmers	1,587	526	1,487	2,233	3,174	1,818
Native born	2,030	541	1,911	2,852	4,680	2,582
Foreign born	1,199	510	1,146	1,747	1,833	1,217
Non-farmers	1,336	476	1,532	2,261	1,878	1,495
Native born	1,840	752	1,988	3,040	2,946	2,639
Foreign born	964	241	1,239	1,679	1,131	668
(The Gini Coefficient, R)						
All persons	0.752	0.832	0.710	0.654	0.722	0.699
Native born	.752	.841	.684	.643	.726	.694
Foreign born	.734	.812	.719	.647	.662	.655
Farmers	.690	.784	.616	.557	.699	.662
Native born	.711	.785	.623	.548	.727	.664
Foreign born	.643	.782	.586	.542	.593	.625
Non-farmers	.832	.884	.807	.785	.764	.776
Native born	.811	.890	.759	.771	.698	.747
Foreign born	.839	.837	.833	.785	.789	.702

[a]Includes those over 69.

Source: See Source for Table 6.

Table 8. Frequency Distributions of Wealth Values for Males 20 and Older, Classified by Age, Nativity, and Occupation, Wisconsin, 1860

Dollar value of lower-class limit	Age					
	20 & up	20–29	30–30	40–49	50–59	60–69
	(The ratio of the number of adult males in the cell in 1860 to the number of adult males in Wisconsin in 1860)					
All males						
0–	0.288	0.166	0.058	0.025	0.015	0.013
1–	.041	.013	.006	.006	.003	.003
100–	.062	.020	.023	.010	.005	.003
200–	.751	.064	.090	.053	.026	.015
1,000–	.358	.046	.117	.105	.059	.024
	1.000^a	0.311^a	0.301^a	0.199	0.108	0.059^a
Native-born farmers						
0–	.070	.045	.011	.004	.003	.002
1–	.005	.003	.001	.001	.000	.001
100–	.012	.005	.003	.002	.001	.000
200–	.056	.020	.019	.009	.007	.005
1,000–	.136	.016	.040	.040	.023	.010
	0.279	0.089	0.075^a	0.055^a	0.035^a	0.018
Foreign-born farmers						
0–	.080	.043	.015	.007	.004	.006
1–	.008	.003	.003	.001	.000	.000
100–	.016	.004	.006	.003	.002	.002
200–	.087	.018	.031	.020	.012	.006
1,000–	.127	.015	.038	.039	.022	.009
	0.319^a	0.084^a	0.094^a	0.070	0.039^a	0.023
Native-born non-farmers						
0–	.054	.034	.009	.005	.002	.002
1–	.008	.003	.003	.001	.000	.000
100–	.014	.005	.004	.003	.001	.001
200–	.040	.012	.016	.008	.003	.001
1,000–	.055	.009	.020	.015	.007	.003
	0.171	0.064^a	0.052	0.032	0.014^a	0.008^a
Foreign-born non-farmers						
0–	.085	.043	.021	.009	.006	.003
1–	.019	.006	.007	.003	.002	.001
100–	.020	.006	.009	.003	.002	.001
200–	.063	.013	.026	.015	.005	.003
1,000–	.044	.006	.017	.012	.005	.002
	0.232^a	0.075^a	0.080	0.042	0.020	0.011^a

[a]Figures in these columns do not add to totals because of rounding.

Source: See Source for Table 6.

We have seen that nativity classification had much, and occupation little, to do with wealth averages. The opposite is true for inequality. Nativity classifications had little bearing on the results of the Gini coefficients but R_F is significantly less than R_{NF}. The main finding is that $R_F - R_{NF} = 0.69 - 0.83$, giving an R_{all} of 0.75. In the case of farmers, one finds that R decreases to 0.55 for those in the age class 40–49 and this might be considered a minimum that could arise with proper allocation of land among farmers. Inequality is at its highest among the young.

Some better understanding of manpower utilization and inequality may be obtained from the figures of Table 8. As recorded, 29 per cent of individuals had no wealth. This situation was dominated by the age group 20–29, where more than 50 per cent were without wealth. The per cent of propertyless individuals dropped substantially for the group from 30–39, particularly for farmers. Only the foreign-born non-farm group had more than 20 per cent without property in this age range.[2] The Gini coefficient is strongly affected by zero cases:

	Gini R before and after elimination of zero cases	
	Before	After
All persons	0.752	0.653
Native born	.752	.618
Foreign born	.734	.659
Farmers	.690	.581
Native born	.711	.614
Foreign born	.643	.524
Non-farmers	.832	.743
Native born	.811	.724
Foreign born	.839	.745

Finally, one notes that the Milwaukee County values presented in Chapter 2 were all more extreme than those in our present tables. The mean wealth was $2,380 for all, $7,100 for native born, and $1,300 for foreign born. The Gini R was 0.893, or more than 10 per cent greater than among non-farm groups in the entire state.

Tables 6, 7, and 8 were based on a sample of size 9,542. It is possible to compute multiple regression coefficients from these cases in attempting further to simplify relationships and to facilitate comparisons to 1850 and 1870 data:

$$\log W = 1.1558 + 0.0314 \text{ age} - 0.2597\ NF - 0.2067\ FB \qquad r^2 = 0.09,$$
$$ (0.0010) \qquad\quad (0.0281) \qquad\quad (0.0275)$$

or $W = \$14.32(1.075)^{age} (0.437)^{NF} (0.621)^{FB}$,

where NF is the ratio of non-farmers to the total population and FB

is the ratio of foreign born to the total population. (Persons with no wealth were assigned values of $10 in logarithmic transformations.) Holding occupation constant and using age 35 as a middle age leads to $W(age, NF, FB) = W(35, k, O) = W(41.6, k, l)$, or a lead of only 6.6 years for native born over foreign born. $W(35, O, k) = W(46.5, l, k)$, or a lead of 11.5 years of farmers over non-farmers. This analysis is somewhat contrary to that obtained from the cross-classification tables because of weighting. The many cases from age 20–29 make our age-differential rate higher than if the number of cases from 20–29 had been the same as for other groups. Likewise, the same age-differential is used for both nativity and occupation.

A more exhaustive analysis is shown in Table 9. Average apparent growth rates in the decade prior to 1860 were 50 per cent or more a

Table 9. Wealth Differentials within Various Age Groups Among Males 20 and Older, Classified by Occupation and Nativity, Wisconsin, 1860[a]

Using log W = log a + log b (age)

Nativity and occupation	Age					
	20 & up	20–29	30–39	40–49	50–59	60–69
	(b, the average ratio of wealth of a person of age t + 1 to one of age t)					
All	1.078	1.537	1.185	1.091	1.003	0.979
Native-born farmers	1.088	1.700	1.192	1.903	0.990	0.986
Foreign-born farmers	1.061	1.560	1.196	1.063	0.972	0.912
Native-born non-farmers	1.095	1.526	1.145	1.086	0.933	1.101
Foreign-born non-farmers	1.062	1.383	1.127	1.120	1.072	0.933

[a]The 30 values were obtained by running 30 separate least-squares analyses for the sample subsets listed in the top portion of Table 7. The ratio for the 212 sample cases of those 70 and older was 0.995. Standard errors of log b were less than half of log b except for those age classes 50 years and older.

Source: See Source to Table 6.

year for a young man in his 20's, 15–20 per cent for one in his 30's, and 6–12 per cent if in his 40's. No wealth accumulation took place after this point for the average person. One finds that the 6.0–6.2 per cent "life-time" rate for foreign born is similar to that in Milwaukee County. The native-born rate of 9 per cent is a little higher than in Milwaukee. There is a difference in methods of weighting for Wisconsin as compared to that for the Milwaukee data of Chapter 2.

The four equations for nativity and occupation can give time-lag differences of wealth of one group to another. The lag of FB behind NB is 38.5 - 35.0 = 3.5 years among farmers, and 46.7 - 35.0 = 11.7 years among non-farmers. The lag of non-farmers behind farmers is

41.2 - 35.0 = 6.2 years among native born and 52.7 - 35.0 = 17.7 years among foreign born. The native-born and foreign-born differential of 30 years found for Milwaukee is not found in the state as a whole in 1860 when one uses data from an unstratified sample where the micro-component is the individual.

B. A STRATIFIED SAMPLE OF WEALTHHOLDINGS OF INDIVIDUALS IN WISCONSIN AND ITS COUNTIES

An exhaustive sample of wealth values was taken in each of Wisconsin's counties, yielding a combined sample for the state of size 47,931. This allows study of wealth dispersion with socio-economic variables which were published on a county basis. The sampling procedure was conducted by stratifying by wealth unless the county was small enough to sample completely. Before presenting the county results, we shall first examine briefly the aggregate distribution for the state, obtained by combining the results for the various counties. The similarity of the overall figures for this sample and those of the non-stratified sample previously given will be noted. In addition, we can demonstrate the great regularity of class frequencies, give detail about the rich, and provide sex classifications not previously presented. Table 10 shows the frequency distribution of the complete enumeration of all wealthholders above $20,000 or more for the entire state and for those having $5,000 or more for the state, but excluding Milwaukee County. Details of the sampling procedure are stated in the note to the table. As it happens, the means, the Gini coefficients, and the number of zero cases are almost the same in Table 10 as they were for Table 6. This was not quite so true for the 1850 results because of illegibility.

It can be seen that Milwaukee County dominates the top part of the distribution, having 105 of the 215 wealthholders above $60,000. The 46 individuals above $100,000 in Milwaukee County were larger in number than the 40 above $100,000 in the rest of the state. Of the 40, there were 11, 6, and 6, respectively, from Rock, Racine, and Dane counties. The table also gives distributions of wealthholdings of women and boys. Since women with wealth constituted only 3 per cent of cases and 3 per cent of aggregate wealth, one is not really forced to study them. It does happen that their mean and dispersion are about the same as that among adult males. The number of boys under 20 with reported wealth is negligible. Further discussion of the shape of the Wisconsin wealth distribution in 1860 will be presented in Chapter 4 and again in Chapter 6 where wealth distributions for later years are given.

Information concerning distributions for each of Wisconsin's 58 counties is listed in part in Table 11. The derived 58 Gini R's will be further analyzed using means compiled from published VEOI figures

Table 10. Distribution of Wealth Among Persons Classified by Sex and Age, Wisconsin, 1860[a]

Lower limit of wealth class in dollars	Males 20 and over		Other Wisconsin groups	
	Wisconsin	Wisconsin (minus Milwaukee County)	Women with wealth	Boys 19 and under with wealth
	(Number of persons)			
0—	60,841	55,134		
1—	2,774	2,254	451	79
50—	5,443	4,643	422	65
100—	6,820	5,600	333	120
120—	795	775	80	8
140—	2,669	2,409	78	39
160—	772	752	36	2
180—	323	323	12	1
200—	7,069	6,309	387	69
250—	2,649	2,569	99	37
300—	5,161	4,821	326	55
350—	2,450	2,370	182	6
400—	4,356	4,076	213	18
450—	2,050	1,930	124	3
500—	7,619	6,839	525	47
600—	6,304	5,784	218	10
700—	5,191	4,951	203	30
800—	4,790	4,690	115	12
900—	3,986	3,766	115	1
1,000—	9,264	8,684	544	6
1,200—	7,533	7,213	292	4
1,400—	5,739	5,599	87	16
1,600—	4,450	4,170	134	2
1,800—	3,718	3,598	158	2
2,000—	8,298	7,938	435	9
2,500—	5,311	5,191	177	37
3,000—	4,478	4,358	251	0
3,500—	3,263	3,043	125	0
4,000—	2,534	2,334	38	1
4,500—	1,894	1,854	77	3
5,000—	2,857	2,577	122	0
6,000	1,905	1,765	46	0
7,000—	1,163	1,043	28	0
8,000—	902	842	27	0
9,000—	600	520	12	1
10,000—	991	871	27	0
12,000—	592	512	8	2
14,000—	356	296	14	2
16,000—	211	191	0	0
18,000—	147	127	7	0
20,000—	356	275	10	0
25,000—	210	165	3	0
30,000—	150	111	1	0
35,000—	67	57	1	0
40,000—	65	47	0	0
45,000—	36	28	0	0

(continued)

Table 10 (continued)

Lower limit of wealth class in dollars	Males 20 and over		Other Wisconsin groups	
	Wisconsin	Wisconsin (minus Milwaukee County)	Women with wealth	Boys 19 and under with wealth
50,000—	97	61	0	0
60,000—	46	22	0	0
70,000—	49	27	0	0
80,000—	22	14	0	0
90,000—	12	7	0	0
100,000—	86	40	1	0
	199,464	183,575	6,544	687
Total wealth (millions)	$289.2	$251.9	$9.11	$.397
$\overline{X}$	$1,450	$1,370	$1,390	$578
Gini R	0.757	0.727	0.621	0.666

[a]This was a sample with a focus on those reporting positive wealth values. First, a few counties were enumerated completely and then a sampling procedure was established, based on the number of males 20 and up in each county. There was a complete enumeration above $0 for 30 counties, above $2,000 for 11 counties, and later $5,000 for 16 counties. Milwaukee's level was $20,000. Below this level, each wealth value from $1 to $1,999 or $1 to $4,999 was counted and 1 in 1, 1 in 5, 1 in 10, 1 in 15, 1 in 20, 1 in 25, and 1 in 30 was selected respectively for counties with adult male populations of 0—1,999; 2,000—2,999; 3,000—4,999; 5,000—6,999; 7,000—8,999; 9,000—10,999; 11,000—12,999. Milwaukee's values come from a sample of 1 in every 20 males from $1 to $19,999 and 1 in 1 above $19,999. For the state, the estimated population of 127,703 items from $1 to $4,999 comes from a sample of size 38,333 items, partly because a few larger counties were sampled completely.

The zero wealth class is a residual class obtained by subtracting the number of wealth holders from the known number of individuals in the county. There is a small problem of the placement of individuals whose ages were unknown. The mean of the 86 males above $100,000 was $180,000.

Source: Schedule 1 of the 1860 Census.

rather than using our stratified sample means. The preference for these VEOI data stems from the fact that they were obtained by adding individual wealth figures in each county.[3]

C. A COUNTY ANALYSIS USING INDEXES
OF ECONOMIC DEVELOPMENT

The fact that the individual wealth declaration of each individual was totalled for all residents of each county is useful for the study of wealth data. These VEOI data have been stated as averages per adult male, obtained by dividing the aggregate for the county by the male population age 20 and older. This VEOI average for the county will be used extensively in this section; it will be called wealth and will be

Exhibit 7
Average[a] Value of Estate Owned (Wealth) for Each of the 58 Counties[b] in 1860

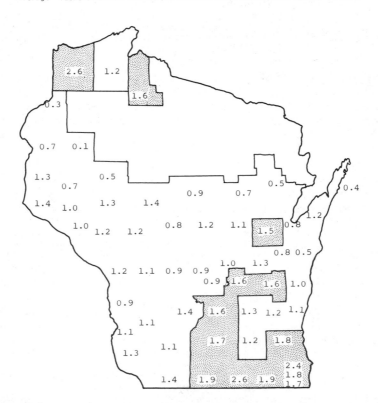

[a]The average is the value of estate owned, obtained from Schedule 1 of
the 1860 census, divided by the number of males 20 years and older. It is
stated in thousands of dollars.
      [b]Shaded counties are those which were above the state average of $1,478.

Source: See Table 11.

given the symbol W. The average wealth for each county is plotted on
the map of Exhibit 7. It is immediately seen that the highest values
are in the southeastern part of the state. These areas include the
cities of Kenosha, Racine, Milwaukee, Beloit, Janesville, and Madison.
An exception to the pattern was the wealthiest group in the state, in
the Duluth-Superior area of Douglas County, where 263 adult males
were very affluent. Aside from this county and a few others, those
areas of above-average wealth were in general the same areas as
those with below-average wages.

The least-squares regression equations involving wealth and wage
rates[4] are:

$$\log Y_{FH} = 1.7077 - 0.1819 \log W, \quad n = 32, \quad r^2 = -0.15$$
$$(0.0797)$$

$$\log Y_{DL} = 0.6833 - 0.2191 \log W, \quad n = 32, \quad r^2 = -0.18$$
$$(0.0859)$$

$$\log Y_{Carp} = 0.6711 - 0.1127 \log W, \quad n = 32, \quad r^2 = -0.03,$$
$$(0.1127)$$

where Y_{FH}, Y_{DL}, and Y_{Carp} are the wages of farm hands, day labor-ers, and carpenters, and W is wealth as defined above. The remarkable phenomenon is that all three equations show a negative relationship between wage rates and wealth. The relationship is so strong in the case of day laborers that a county with 10 per cent more average wealth than another paid 2.2 per cent less per day to laborers. A tentative conclusion on the basis of these data is that income inequality in the hinterland, the very frontier of settlement, might be less than in the more established areas. The conclusion would stem from the assertion that wage rates represent lower income groups, and that wealth aver-ages largely represent the income of high income groups.

It is desirable to investigate the proposition that counties with higher wealth averages are those that were more developed. Perhaps the best indication of county development is density of population. It is almost an index of urbanization. Counties at the frontier running in a line west from Green Bay had densities as low as 1 person per square mile while Milwaukee County had 261 persons per square mile. Table 11 has a division of the 56 effective counties into three groups, the highest group having more than 10 times as many persons per square mile as the lowest group. The lowest, with density $D < 4.0$, include the three northern counties of Douglas, Ashland, and La Pointe (Bay-field) and nine counties in the belt west of Green Bay.

One might briefly note the characteristics of the variables of Table 11 as a first step. The more urban areas ($D > 40$) have relatively: fewer single and more family men; higher wealth per person; older adult males; more foreign born in the population; fewer adults in manu-facturing than in frontier counties; the same manufacturing cost per employee in manufacturing; lower wages to farm hands, day laborers, and carpenters; more church accommodations per person; more farms per adult male; greater improved acreage per farm; higher cash value of farms per acre; more land in farms; and middle inequality levels of wealth between the higher levels of the underdeveloped ($D < 4.0$) and the lower levels of the middle developed ($4.0 < D < 40$) groups. There is essentially a U-shaped pattern for measures of inequality of wealth and land in the table.

Let us examine more closely the relationship between average wealth and density for the various counties. Exhibit 8 illustrates the relationship in detail. It is immediately apparent that the three coun-ties with the smallest densities did not fit the scheme. These were Douglas, Ashland, and La Pointe (Bayfield) counties. Douglas county includes the entrance to the Wisconsin River. Ashland and Bayfield

Table 11. Indexes of Development for Fifty-Six Counties, Classified by
Population Density, Wisconsin, 1860

Development Index Z	Correlation coefficient	Density, D = Number persons per square mile			
		$D < 4.0$ (12 counties)	$4.0 \leq D < 40$ (30 counties)	$D \geq 40$ (14 counties)	All D (56 counties)
	$r(N=56)$[a]	(Arithmetic mean of the 12, 30, 14, and 56 values)[a]			
Density, D, or persons per square mile in 1860	1.00	1.7	17.7	67.1	26.6
Ratio of number of males 20 & up to number of all males, 1860	-0.59[a]	0.335	.269	0.249	0.278
Arithmetic mean of wealth per male 20 & up in 1860 (Table 3, p. 33)	0.33	$1,069	$1,151	$1,597	$1,245
Median age of males 20 & up in 1860	0.69[a]	32.3	35.5	37.2	35.3
Ratio of number of foreign born to number of all persons in 1860	0.30[a]	0.305	0.324	0.371	0.331
Ratio of number of hands employed in manufacturing to adult males, 1860	-0.36[a]	0.209	0.060	0.075	0.096
Average annual cost of labor per employee in manufacturing, 1860	0.06	$279	$266	$287	$274
Average monthly wage to a farm hand in 1860	-0.72	$17.44	$13.88	$12.07	$14.48
Average to a daylaborer without board in 1860	-0.55	$1.25	$1.03	$0.86	
Average to a carpenter without board in 1860	-0.60	$2.21	$1.62	$1.28	$1.71
Ratio of number of church accommodations to total number of persons	0.44[a]	0.20	0.30	0.42	0.32
Ratio of number of farms to number of adult males in 1860	0.48[a]	0.154	0.358	0.371	0.318
Number of acres of improved land per farm in 1860	0.44	37	41	57	44
Cash value of farms per acre of improved & unimproved farm land, 1850	0.64	$9.00	$11.01	$22.72	$13.51
Ratio of number of acres of improved to improved plus unimproved farm land in 1860	0.76[a]	0.213	0.329	0.578	0.366
Proportion of land area in improved and unimproved farm land, 1860	0.83[a]	0.239	0.321	0.771	0.370

(continued)

Table 11 (continued)

Development Index Z	Corre-lation coeffi-cient	Density, D = Number persons per square mile			
		$D < 4.0$ (12 counties)	$4.0 \leq D < 40$ (30 counties)	$D \geq 40$ (14 counties)	All D (56 counties)
Arithmetic mean of wealth per male 20 & up in 1860[b]	0.33	$1,036	$1,140	$1,537	$1,199
Gini R of wealth in real & personal estate of males 20 & up, 1860[b]	-0.14	0.762	0.681	0.723	0.709
Gini R of non-zero values of wealth of males 20 & up, 1860[b]	-0.21	0.640	0.561	0.601	0.588
Proportion of adult males with zero wealth in 1860	0.07[a]	0.332	0.281	0.308	0.298
Gini R of farm acreage including an estimate of landless adult males $(=L_{land})$, 1860	-0.43	0.907	0.767	0.758	0.795
Gini R of farm acreage $(=R_{farm})$, 1860	0.06	0.394	0.354	0.359	0.364
Gini R of wealth of adult males, $(=R_W)$ in 1870[c]	-0.30	0.770	0.657	0.697	0.691
Gini R of farm acreage including landless adult males $(=R_{land})$, 1870	-0.31	0.776	0.729	0.709	0.734
Ratio of number of farms per adult male, 1870[c]	0.26[a]	0.303	0.474	0.389	0.416
Density, D, or persons per square mile in 1960	0.66	33	60	189	86
Arithmetic mean income per adult male in 1959	0.57	$3,607	$3,871	$4,976	$4,091
Gini R of income values of adult males in 1959	-0.38	0.427	0.435	0.383	0.420

[a]From $Z = a + b \log D$. Others are from $\log Z = c + d \log D$. $N = 56$, except 32 for entries 8, 9, and 10; 47 for entry 11.
[b]Based on a sample of Schedule 1 of the 1860 Census.
[c]"Adult" is males 21 years old and older.

Source: Manuscript analyses of the 1860 census, in the possession of the author.

counties had, respectively, 145 and 119 adult males, largely native-born persons. The per cent of foreign born in those two areas ranked 54th and 56th among the 56 counties.

If the 12 counties with lowest densities are eliminated (see Exhibit 8):

$$\log W = 2.8136 + 0.2023 \log D, \quad n = 44, \quad r^2 = 0.25$$
$$(0.0538)$$

Exhibit 8
Average Wealth Related to Population Density for 56 Counties in Wisconsin in 1860

Wealth per adult
male, in dollars

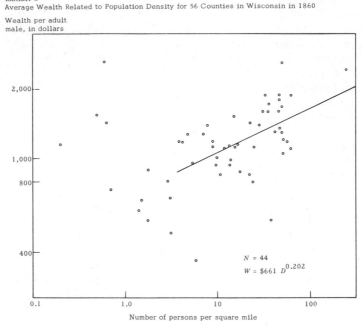

Number of persons per square mile

Source: See Table 11.

$$W = \$661 \; D^{.20} = \$661(1.020)^t \quad \text{if } D = 1.097^t$$

$$\log W = 2.9301 + 0.2631 \log D - 0.5907 \; FB, \quad n = 44, \quad r^2 = 0.47$$
$$ (0.0481)$$

$$W = \$851(1.025)^t (0.257)^{FB} \quad \text{if } D = 1.097^t$$

$$FB = 0.1989 + 0.1029 \log D, \quad n = 44, \quad r^2 = 0.09,$$
$$ (0.0494)$$

where D is the number of persons per square mile and FB is the proportion of foreign born in the total population. A county with 10 per
cent more population than another had, on the average, a per capita
wealth 2 per cent higher. Although these figures are for a given point
in time, it is possible to speculate about the ramifications of the results over time. If a county's population increased 10 per cent, might
not its per capita wealth increase 2 per cent? If its population growth
were 6 per cent per annum, might not its per capita wealth increase by
1.2 per cent per annum? Wisconsin's population grew 9.7 per cent
per annum from 1850 to 1860, on the average. If we could think of an
average county as growing at this rate with county A beginning a year
ahead of county B, then its wealth would be 2 per cent larger. This
may be consistent with the findings of Chapter 2 where it was found
that the data had an implied productivity increase of 2 per cent a year.

This formulation implies that population growth necessitates economic growth, which is ridiculous. It is the fact that the data reflect economic growth accompanied by population growth which allows one to interpret the data by means of a population growth category. The two ideas may be stated more formally as $Y = aD^{0.2}$ and $D = 1.10^t$. Then $Y = a(1.10^t)^{0.2} = a(1.02)^t$. If one had guessed at the relationships shown in Exhibit 8, assuming an average value for population growth in 1860, the answer would probably have been the correct one. The above arguments are somewhat tenuous. Those counties with greater densities will not grow 10 per cent a year. On the other hand, the slope of 0.2 for the WD elasticity is subject to qualifications. Counties with low densities had a smaller per cent foreign born than those with high densities. If the foreign born did not enter the high-density counties, average wealth growth would be larger.

There is one sense in which population growth does increase wealth, and this is by increasing the demand for land. We now investigate this problem at some length, using several variables. The level of average wealth is highly related to that of the cash value of farm land per acre, CV. CV, in turn, is very strongly related to density, as is shown in Exhibit 9:

$$\log W = 2.0668 + 0.9690 \log CV, \quad n = 44, \quad r^2 = 0.57$$
$$(0.1343)$$

Exhibit 9
The Value[a] of Farm Land in Relation to Population Density for 44 Counties[b] in Wisconsin in 1860

Value of farm land
in dollars per acre

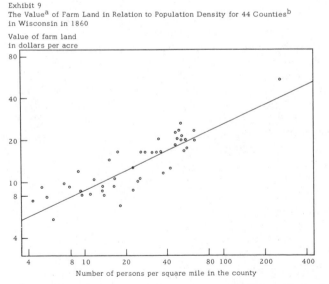

Number of persons per square mile in the county

[a]Average cash value is based on improved and unimproved land.
[b]Counties with densities of less than four persons per square mile are not shown.

Source: See Table 11.

$$\log CV = 0.9550 + 0.4624 \log D, \quad n = 44, \quad r^2 = 0.78$$
$$(0.0384)$$

and $CV = \$9.02\,(1.044)^t$ if $D = 1.097^t$.

An index of rural development is the ratio of improved acreage in farms to improved plus unimproved acreage in farms for each county. This variable, I, pertains only to that land in the county which is actually farm land or land in farms. In certain underdeveloped counties this may be a small proportion of total land area. It will be shown that I and D are positively correlated:

$$\log D = 0.6216 + 1.8021\,I, \quad n = 44, \quad r^2 = 0.59$$
$$(0.2317)$$

$$\log CV = 0.7098 + 1.0053\,I, \quad n = 44, \quad r^2 = 0.67$$
$$(0.1099)$$

$$\log CV = 0.5078 + 0.4197\,I + 0.3249 \log D, \quad n = 44, \quad r^2 = 0.82$$
$$(0.1265) \quad\ (0.0539)$$

$$CV = \$3.22\,(2.63)^I\,(1.031)^t \quad \text{if} \quad D = 1.097^t.$$

It is perhaps of merit first to examine the consequences of no improved land ($I = 0$) and no unimproved land ($I = 1$). At $I = 0$, $CV = \$5.12$, which is very substantially above the pre-emption price of $\$1.25$. At $I = 1$, $CV = \$51.90$, or $\$190$ at 1966 consumer prices. $CV(I = 1)/CV(I = 0) = 10.1$ and $D\,(I = 1)/D\,(I = 0) = 44$ years if $D = (1.097)^t$. Hypothetically, it would take 44 years for CV to have increased to 10 times its original value, at an average annual rate of increase of 5.4 per cent a year. This chain of reasoning, using I and D, yields an answer similar to the former one without using I of 4.4 per cent. For the equation $CV = f(I, D)$ we have a hypothetical estimate of the increase in CV to 2.63 times its original value if population did not increase. We also have a net regression coefficient for t of 1.031 instead of 1.044, or 1.054 for the hypothetical situation of no improvement of land. Might two thirds of the increase in cash value be due to population increases and one third to improvement?

Many other possible relationships between W and the development indexes of Table 11 were of interest. Even the number of church accommodations per person, C, was related to wealth by the equation:

$$C = -1.1767 + 0.4907 \log W, \quad n = 47, \quad r^2 = 0.23.$$
$$(0.1332)$$

The variable, I, serves as a good proxy for the variable, S, which is the proportion of land in the county reported as farm land, where $r^2(S, I) =$

0.72 for $n = 56$. A more systematic treatment might include a factor analysis. One relatively unrefined capital function is

$$\log W = 1.5420 + 0.5107 \log CV + 0.4013 \log CL, \quad n = 44, \quad r^2 = 0.62$$
$$(0.0768)(0.1457)$$

$$W = \$34.80 \; CV^{0.51} CL^{0.40},$$

where CL is the average annual cost of labor per employee. A given percentage increase in wages would necessitate almost as much of an increase in capital as the same percentage increase in the cash value of a farm.

One possible check may be made of the data of the first section of this chapter, using individuals in the state as the microcomponents, and the data of this section, using the 56 counties as microcomponents. From the former we have:

$$\log W = 0.9692 + 0.0327 \; age - 0.2274 \; FB, \quad n = 9,542, \quad r^2 = 0.10$$
$$(0.0011)(0.0277)$$

$$W = \$9.32 \, (1.078)^{age} (0.599)^{FB}.$$

For our 56, we may consider the median age of males 20 years old and over in each county and the proportion of foreign born among the total population of the country:

$$\log W = 2.3230 + 0.0257 \; age - 0.4965 \; FB, \quad n = 56, \quad r^2 = 0.20$$
$$(0.0089)(0.1768)$$

$$W = \$210 \, (1.061)^{age} (0.319)^{FB}.$$

The 9,542 equation gives $W(age, FB) = W(35, 0) = W(41.8, 1)$ and the 56 equation gives $W(age, FB) = W(35, 0) = W(54.3, 1)$. The difference in the average growth rates of 7.8 and 6.1 per cent is not serious. The difference in time lags of 6.8 years and 19.3 years is serious. It would have been most desirable for the lag to have been 30 years, as it was in Milwaukee. The spiral model of Chapter 2 might then have been applied to the whole state with more efficacy. Unfortunately, the lag for the state as a whole was not over 20 years and was probably not over 7 years. One must place more reliance on the latter figure because it is tied more closely to actual individuals and gives greater weights to counties with more people. The assertion can be made that inequality in Milwaukee would more closely approach that of the rest of the state as the proportion of foreign born decreased. It is recalled that in 1860 the Gini R for Milwaukee was 0.89 and that for the state outside of Milwaukee was 0.72.

The conclusion in general is that average wealth is a good proxy for economic growth. Was there then much area inequality in Wisconsin, if area is defined as a county rather than as a smaller ethnic area? A Lorenz curve can be constructed from the data which will measure county inequality. The 56 counties are first arrayed from highest to lowest on the basis of per capita wealth, W. Then the number of persons, $\bar{L}_W$, are cumulated with their total wealth, $\bar{P}_W$, assuming each individual in a county had a wealth figure equivalent to the average wealth of the county. The assumption is thus made that there is no dispersion within the county. This measure for Wisconsin in 1860 has a concentration coefficient, R, of 0.1928. It would be presumed that this measure would be very close to zero if there had been uniform development in the 56 counties. One should not, however, neglect the idea of smaller areas with groups of foreign-born or native-born elements in them.[5]

We turn now to an analysis of the level of inequality in each county, using Gini R computations developed in section B of the present chapter. It is noted in Exhibit 10 that inequality was greatest in the most sparsely settled areas and again in the most urban areas in the southeastern part of the state. The belt west of Green Bay is conspicuous for its inequality of wealth since the level is often 20 to 30 per cent higher than that of counties south of the belt. Is this a sign that inequality on the frontier was higher? Perhaps not, because of the fertility of the soil and the weather.

Our 1850 data of Chapter 4, dealing with the frontier when it was further south, will have more cogency. Then there was logic for the case that the initial turmoil in acquiring land left many persons propertyless and created a transient situation of large farmland inequality. But the 1860 situation is one in which the high inequality belt west of Green Bay lies where the soil pattern changes. A map with a clear dividing line for soil types in the high inequality range is shown in a publication of the Land Economics Institute.[6] Snow covers the ground in this area from 100 to 140 days a year. "Poor soils are often intermixed with good soils—a fact that was partly responsible for failures by many settlers who were unfortunate in their choice of land."[7] The counties with $D < 4$ were likely to be ones in non-farm areas with less than half as many farms per adult male as existed in other areas and with a greater per cent of persons engaged in forest activities.

Some regression equations involving R_W as the dependent variable are:

$$\log R_W = -0.1403 - 0.0114 \log D, \quad D > 0, \quad n = 56, \quad r^2 = 0.02$$
$$(0.0110)$$

$$\log R_W = -0.2152 + 0.0396 \log D, \quad D > 4, \quad n = 44, \quad r^2 = 0.08$$
$$(0.0709)$$

Exhibit 10
The Gini Coefficient of Inequality[a] of Wealth among Persons in Each
of 56 Counties in Wisconsin in 1860

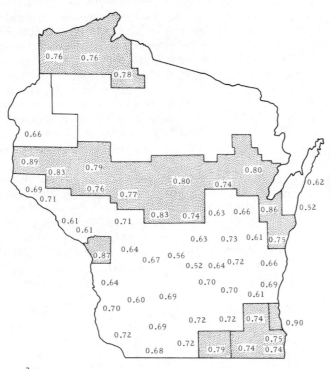

[a]Shaded areas have $R \geq 0.74$

Source: Schedule 1 of the 1860 Census.

$$\log R_W = -0.2909 + 0.0451 \log W, \quad D > 0, \quad n = 56, \quad r^2 = 0.02$$
$$(0.0414)$$

$$\log R_W = -0.5738 + 0.1335 \log W, \quad D > 4, \quad n = 44, \quad r^2 = 0.15$$
$$(0.0492)$$

$$\log R_W = 0.2933 - 0.0135 \, age + 0.0163 \, FB + 0.0223 \log D, \quad D > 0,$$
$$(0.0037) \qquad (0.0553) \qquad (0.0141)$$
$$n = 56, \quad r^2 = 0.22$$

$$\log R_W = 0.4488 - 0.0206 \, age + 0.0043 \, FB + 0.0963 \log D, \quad D > 4,$$
$$(0.0047) \qquad (0.0554) \qquad (0.0218)$$
$$n = 44, \quad r^2 = 0.38.$$

One can say that inclusion of the belt west of Green Bay means that inequality is little associated with density or average wealth. Exclusion of this belt indicates a positive relationship between wealth inequality and urbanity, between wealth inequality and the average level of wealth. R_W is negatively correlated with age and United States nativity. Regression equations for R_W are generally not more explanatory when employees in manufacturing and day labor rates are included.

Our index, R_{land}, has a high relationship with R_W. One first computes R_{farm}, the inequality of farmland, from the available distribution of farms, classified by the number of acres of improved land in 1860. An estimate is then made of the number of landless persons by subtracting the number of farms from the number of males 20 years old and over in the county. These are considered landless persons having no acreage:

$$R_{land} = R_{farms} \begin{bmatrix} \text{proportion of} \\ \text{farms to males} \\ \text{20 and up} \end{bmatrix} + 1 - \begin{bmatrix} \text{proportion of} \\ \text{farms to males} \\ \text{20 and up} \end{bmatrix}$$

$$= 1 + \begin{bmatrix} \text{proportion of} \\ \text{farms to males} \\ \text{20 and up} \end{bmatrix} \begin{bmatrix} R_{farm} - 1 \end{bmatrix}$$

$$\log R_W = 0.5260 + 0.6145 \log R_{land}, \quad n = 56, \quad r^2 = 0.58$$
$$(0.0709)$$

$$\log R_W = 0.5467 + 0.6314 \log R_{land}, \quad n = 44, \quad r^2 = 0.54.$$
$$(0.0899)$$

The scatter diagram for this situation is shown in Exhibit 11. By the nature of the formula for R_{land}, one would expect the following high correlations:

$$\log R_{land} = 0.0683 + 0.1071 \log R_{farms} - 0.3903 \begin{bmatrix} \text{proportion of} \\ \text{farms to males} \\ \text{20 and up} \end{bmatrix},$$
$$(0.0184) \qquad\qquad\qquad (0.0140)$$
$$n = 56, \quad r^2 = 0.90.$$

$$\log (number\ of\ zero\text{-}wealth\ males) = 8.9324 +$$
$$0.6676 \log (number\ of\ farms), \quad n = 56, \quad r^2 = 0.69$$
$$(0.0616)$$

$$\log R_{land} = -0.0673 - 0.1000 (proportion\ of\ total\ area\ in\ farms),$$
$$(0.0248)$$
$$n = 56, \quad r^2 = 0.23.$$

Exhibit 11
Land Inequality Related to Wealth Inequality for 56 Counties in Wisconsin
in 1860

Wealth coefficient
of concentration
for the county[a]

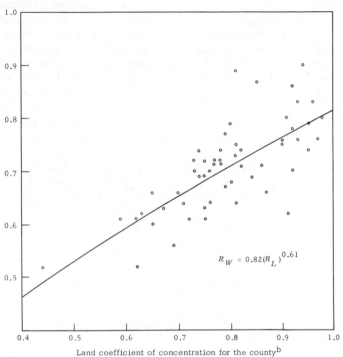

$$R_W = 0.82(R_L)^{0.61}$$

Land coefficient of concentration for the county[b]

[a]Of the distribution of wealth among all males 20 years old and over.
[b]Of the distribution of improved farm land among all males 20 years old and
over.

Source: See Table 11.

Lest one overemphasize zero cases, it should be remembered that even
after eliminating zero cases, there is still an inequality problem:

$$\log R_W = -0.0072 + 0.6164 \log R_W, \text{ non-zero, } n = 56, \ r^2 = 0.68.$$
$$(0.0579)$$

We have found from the Wisconsin wealth figures in 1860 an exten-
sive apparent growth rate similar to that which was given for Milwaukee in Chapter 2. This rate was 6 to 8 per cent when associated with
age and 2 per cent per capita when associated with the population
density of counties. Average wealth of native born was roughly twice

that of foreign born, depending on the variables and areas included in
the analysis, thus giving a lead time much less than 30 years. Surprisingly, non-farmers from age 30 to 50 had average wealth higher
than that of farmers. Wealth was highly correlated with land values
and these with population density and, to a lesser degree, with the
extent that land was improved.

The Gini coefficient for Wisconsin wealth was a substantial figure
of 0.75, being 0.69 for farmers, 0.83 for non-farmers, and 0.72 when
Milwaukee County is excluded. It is remembered that the Milwaukee
coefficient was 0.89. One cannot obtain a clear-cut answer to the
question of whether or not inequality in 1860 was greater on the frontier than in the more densely populated areas because of certain pecu-
liarities of Wisconsin geography. There was a band of counties running west from Green Bay, at the edge of desirable farm land and climate, which had high inequality. These may not be thought of as a
proper extension of the agricultural frontier. The relationship between
county inequality and population density is weakly negative if these
counties are included, weakly positive if excluded. It will be seen in
the next chapter that the results are much clearer in 1850, when the
frontier was further south, and in 1870, when immigrant and migrant
farmers without land were not relatively so important. County inequality in 1860 was greater, but highly correlated with inequality of farm
land holdings and the per cent of persons without land. Finally, there
is some little evidence that county wealth inequality and income inequality were negatively related in 1860, based on the inverse relationship between wage rates and wealth.

Chapter 4

Inequality in 1850 and 1870

We are studying the distribution of wealth and income in the early development of Milwaukee and Wisconsin. The most complete body of information for these areas stems from the distributions for 1860. Almost all of the conclusions of Chapter 6 concerning long-run changes from the nineteenth to the twentieth centuries are based on the 1860 data. One would be negligent, however, if he did not investigate figures that are available for the years 1850 and 1870. Persons were asked the value of their real estate holdings in 1850 (as distinguished from the real estate plus personal estate values asked for in the 1860 and 1870 censuses). The data from the census of 1870 for Wisconsin, but particularly for Milwaukee, proved to be somewhat disappointing even though measures of relative dispersion are meaningful. Absolute values in 1870 are questionable for Milwaukee, since reported wealth per capita did not increase as much as prices from 1860 to 1870.

A. THE DISTRIBUTION OF REAL ESTATE IN 1850 IN MILWAUKEE COUNTY

One is able to obtain from the 1850 census figures a general conception of wealth distribution in Milwaukee County only 12 to 15 years after settlement had begun. A sample of 1850 is presented in Table 12; it reveals extreme inequality of holdings. Two thirds of males age 20 and up reported no real estate owned. Even among the one third reporting real estate, the concentration coefficient was 0.701. Among all males, the coefficient was 0.908. The top 1 per cent of males held 45 per cent of the total value of real estate. That portion of the Lorenz curve which is germane is presented in Exhibit 12.

In order to have a direct comparison with data for 1860, it was necessary to take an additional sample of real estate holdings in the later

Table 12. Distribution of the Value of Real Estate Owned Among Males
            20 Years Old and Over, Milwaukee County, 1850 and 1860

Lower limit of wealth class in dollars X	Wealth in real estate in 1850			Wealth in real estate in 1860		
	Total number of males in the wealth class	N_X or the per cent of total males above the lower limit, X	P_X or the per cent of total wealth above the lower limit, X	Total number of males in the wealth class	N_X or the per cent of total males above the lower limit, X	P_X or the per cent of total wealth above the lower limit, X
0–	6,010	100.0	100.0	8,370	100.0	100.0
50–	90	33.4	100.0	150	47.7	100.0
100–	310	32.4	99.9	320	46.8	99.9
200–	750	28.9	99.3	1,540	44.8	99.8
500–	640	20.6	95.5	1,350	35.1	98.2
1,000–	650	13.6	88.7	1,400	26.7	95.4
2,000–	330	6.40	75.4	1,540	18.0	89.8
5,000–	139	2.74	61.1	790	8.33	75.3
10,000–	50	1.20	48.2	253	3.40	59.6
20,000–	43	0.64	38.9	179	1.81	50.1
50,000–	9	0.17	22.2	71	.69	35.7
100,000–	5	0.07	13.0	27	.25	23.2
200,000–	1	0.01	3.4	12	.08	14.4
500,000–	0			2	.01	3.3
	9,027			16,004		
Arithmetic mean		$723			$2,072	
Gini coefficient		0.908			0.881	

Source: Schedule 1 of the 1850 and 1860 censuses. The sample for 1850 was obtained
by recording all the presumed 247 real estate values of $5,000 or more. Below this
level, a sample of size 878 was obtained by examining one line in each 10 of the census manuscripts. The sample accounted for 9,027 of the 8,812 males 20 years old and
over published by the census bureau. The sample for 1860 real estate was obtained by
examining all the presumed 544 values of $10,000 or more. A sample of 902 below
$10,000 averaged about one of every 17 adult males. The census count in 1860 was
15,899 adult males.

year. Results are given in Table 12 and in Exhibit 12. We see that
wealth in real estate was, if anything, a little more concentrated in
1850 than it was in 1860. The average value of real estate holdings
increased from $723 to $2,072 in the period we are considering, even
though there was an increase in the percentage of adult males owning
land. Arithmetic mean holdings per land *owner* were $2,163 in 1850
and $4,334 in 1860. Correcting these latter figures for price increases
of 11 per cent, the average annual increase of real estate value in the
ten-year period was 6.1 per cent.

Table 13 has data from selected counties in seven states. These
figures are published in a footnote in the 1850 census almost without

Exhibit 12
Lorenz Curves of the Distribution of Real Estate in 1850 and in 1860,
and Total Estate in 1860 and in 1870 among Males 20 Years Old and
Over in Milwaukee County

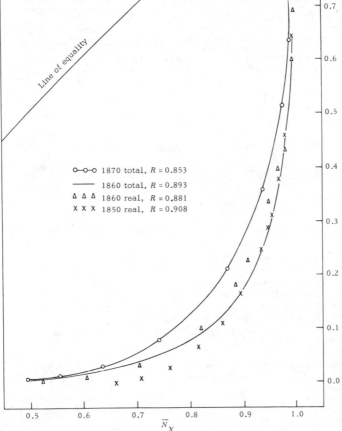

Source: Schedule 1 of the 1850, 1860, and 1870 Censuses.

any description or explanation. The data are for actual holders only.
and may be quixotic since the percentage of non-landowners in the
counties is not considered. It seems that the Milwaukee distribution
has 10 to 20 per cent more concentration than that in the other northern counties and is on a level with that in southern and border-state
counties. Real estate wealth was very highly concentrated in this 15-
year-old county; this concentration decreased slightly in the next 10
years as a greater proportion of adult males became landowners.

Table 13. Distribution of Real Estate Among Real Estate Owners, Milwaukee
County and Counties in Seven Other States, 1850

Lower limit of wealth class in dollars	States containing the counties sampled by Census Bureau							
	Ky.	Mich.	Pa.	R.I.	S.C.	La.[a]	Ohio	Milwaukee
	(Cumulative number of real estate owners above lower class limit)							
100[b]—	907	5,499	1,662	2,833	8,467	2,030	1,927	2,927
1,000—	494	1,900	773	1,808	5,417	1,501	1,101	1,227
5,000—	152	119	101	266	1,831	779	161	247
10,000—	67	29	18	50	953	469	46	108
50,000—	3	1	0	1	98	101	0	15
100,000—	1	0	0	0	21	23	0	6
500,000—	0	0	0	0	1	0	0	0
	(Rough measures of dispersion and central tendency)							
Arithmetic mean[c]	$1,817	531	816	1,152	2,737	6,012	1,067	1,306
Concentration coefficient	0.729	0.606	0.620	0.563	0.735	0.742	0.584	0.774
Pareto slope[d]	−1.35	−1.93	−1.63	−1.92	−1.38	−0.91	−1.38	−1.16

[a]Slaves in this state were most often classified as real estate.
[b]Author assumes this to be the lower limit.
[c]Lower limits have been used as values of the midpoints of the classes in the computation of the mean and the concentration coefficient.
[d]The Pareto slope has been computed from $1,000 to the highest income point.
Slope = $(\log N_{X_1} - \log N_{X_2}) / (\log X_1 - \log X_2)$.

Source: Milwaukee, Schedule 1 of the 1850 Census and Table 12; states, U.S. Census Office. 7th Census, 1850. *Compendium* (GPO: Washington, D.C. 1854), pp. 153, 191.

B. TENUOUS WEALTH DATA FOR MILWAUKEE IN 1870

In the section of Chapter 2 dealing with secrecy, it was pointed out that by VEOA and VEOT measures of wealth for Milwaukee, obtained from public records, one would have expected our VEOI aggregate from Schedule 1 to increase two to three times from 1860 to 1870.

Milwaukee County 1850
VEOI $6,188,000
    (real est. only)
VEOA Unknown
VEOT Unknown

Wisconsin 1850
VEOI $65,700,000
    (estimate of real est. only)
VEOA 26,715,525
VEOT 42,056,595

Milwaukee County 1860		Wisconsin 1860	
VEOI	$38,712,145	VEOI	$294,901,000
VEOA	15,984,000	VEOA	185,944,000
VEOT	22,840,000	VEOT	273,671,000

Milwaukee County 1870		Wisconsin 1870	
VEOI	$65,875,000	VEOI	$625,000,000
VEOA	51,275,000	VEOA	333,209,000
VEOT	88,422,000	VEOT	702,307,000

It was, in effect, only 70 per cent larger, and did not even equal the corrected-assessed or true-value figure. This percentage increase was not so large as that from population growth and inflation, without even considering productivity increases.[1] It may very well be that from the standpoint of absolute levels, our data are deficient. This probably reflects a penalty for heavy income taxation during the 1860's. In 1869 a law was passed prohibiting the publication in newspapers of incomes and names of earners from income tax returns. However, there is some evidence (to be presented in Section D) that some well-to-do persons may have moved into other parts of the state by 1870. It should be remembered that in 1870 Milwaukee County had 80 per cent of adult males who were foreign born while the rest of the state had only 57 per cent foreign-born males.

There is merit in examining our data for relative dispersion. We may operate under the assumption that a constant lie coefficient, or discount factor, is employed in 1870 while making a conscientious market value estimate in 1860. Table 14 gives the distribution for 1870. The data are dominated by the worth of Mr. Alexander Mitchell, President of the Milwaukee and St. Paul Railroad, and by 1869 also President of the Northwestern Railroad. His wealth of $1,832,000 was 0.4 per cent of the aggregate wealth, even though he was only 1 of 22,000 persons in the labor force.

Results for 1860 and 1870 differ. There is first the value for Mr. Mitchell, even more prominent in 1870 than before. Below him there are relatively few values above $100,000. It is not until one gets as low as $5,000 that wealth growth from 1860 to 1870 appears to have benefited any group. In the range from $2,000 to perhaps $200, or near the median, the data do show that 1870 was a better year than 1860. In this latter range, there is enough difference to account for an annual 2 per cent or more increase in wealth, corrected for price changes.

We have, then, some little evidence of a tycoon effect in the very upper tail. Inequality in this region definitely increased. Below $5,000 there is a real improvement. The median value in 1870 is larger than that in 1860. The Gini coefficient of 0.853 for Milwaukee in 1870 is substantially less than the 0.893 value for 1860. There is some little evidence that the position of middle-income groups improved.

Table 14.   Distribution of Wealth Among Males 20 Years Old and Over, Milwaukee County, 1870

Lower limit of the wealth class in dollars X	Total number of males in the wealth class	Total amount of wealth in thousands of dollars in the wealth class	N_X or the per cent of total males above the lower limit, X	A_X or the per cent of total wealth above the lower limit, X	Total number of native-born males in the wealth class	Total number of foreign-born males in the wealth class
			All groups		Nativity groups	
0–						
10–	9,890	0	100.00	100.00	2,408	7,482
20–						
50–	86	4	55.86	100.00	0	86
100–	1,118	122	55.47	99.99	43	1,075
200–	1,376	387	50.48	99.80	129	1,247
500–	1,806	1,239	44.34	99.21	172	1,634
1,000–	2,408	3,355	36.28	97.33	215	2,193
2,000–	2,881	8,718	25.54	92.22	387	2,494
5,000–	1,505	9,937	12.68	78.96	559	946
10,000–	860	10,100	5.96	63.84	430	430
20,000–	272	8,185	2.12	48.47	144	128
50,000–	119	7,902	0.91	36.02	77	42
100,000–	70	9,314	0.38	24.00	44	26
200,000–	13	3,178	0.07	9.82	7	6
500,000–	2	1,450	0.01	4.99	0	2
1,000,000–	1	1,832	0.004	2.79	0	1
	22,407	65,723			4,615	17,792
Arithmetic mean	$2,933				$6,058	$2,122
Median	$ 150				$ 0	$ 200
Gini coefficient	0.853				0.847	0.831

Source: Schedule 1 of the 1870 Census. The sample was obtained by examining all the presumed 477 values of $20,000 or more. A sample of 1 of each 40 lines yielded a sample of 510 adult males below $20,000 which was substantially less than the census count of 22,460 adult males. (It was necessary to estimate the number of 20-year olds using the sample data.) Accordingly, a discrete weighting factor of 43 was applied to each of the 510 cases.

C. AGE AND NATIVITY CLASSIFICATION IN 1870

Even though absolute levels of wealth in Milwaukee in 1870 as obtained from the census are subject to doubt, there may be merit in examining relative levels, such as those between age-nativity classes.

A fair analysis is one where all evidence is presented. We shall look at the data even though results are not quite so clear as one would have hoped.

From 1860 to 1870, Milwaukee County's male population age 20 and up increased at an annual rate of 3.5 per cent. This is a sharp drop from the annual rate of 6.6 per cent in the preceding decade, and one should expect to find some striking changes in the age distributions from the year 1860 to the year 1870.

Exhibit 13 is very important in portraying the shifts in age distribution. The native-born pattern is still exponential with a least-squares line of $Y_{NB} = 239(1.050)^X$, where Y is the frequency per one-year age interval and X is age minus 20. The apparent 1870 population growth of 5 per cent is less than in the preceding decade but still somewhat

Exhibit 13
Number of Native-Born and Foreign-Born Males Classified by Age[a] for Milwaukee County in 1870

Number of males in
one-year interval

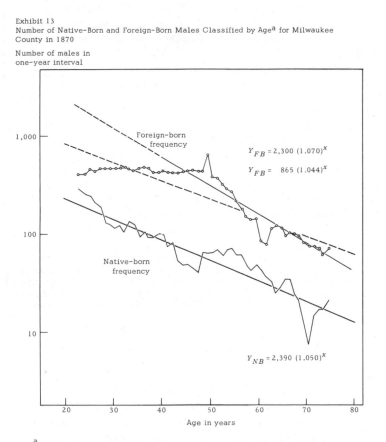

[a]Data for the ages 25 to 69 are 10-year moving averages. Lesser periods have been used in smoothing the data outside this range. The least-squares regression equations have been fitted to 30 and 52 moving average points from ages 40 to 74, and 23 to 74.

Source: Schedule 1 of the 1870 Census.

reflects the apparent rate of 6.3 per cent in 1860. There is a slight youth-frequency gap under age 45 in the 1870 pattern which explains the difference.

It is the foreign-born pattern that has been broken. The frequency remains essentially constant from age 23 to age 45. Only above that level have we a reflection of the 1860 configuration. This absence of the young foreign born has large consequences on the inequality of wealth distribution in 1870. Two lines have been fitted to the foreign-born frequencies. One is: $Y_{FB} = 2,300(1.070)^X$, $40 \leq$ age ≤ 74, and the other is $Y_{FB} = 865(1.044)^X$, $23 \leq$ age ≤ 74. In discussing apparent wealth accumulation, one might use 4.4 per cent as an average to represent foreign-born population growth and 5.0 per cent to represent native-born population growth. More realistic might be the actual average annual per cent of increase from 1860 to 1870 of 4.6 for native born and 3.5 for foreign born. In any case, our 1860 model has become distorted in many ways. Our 30-year differential still holds, that is $Y_{FB}(X) = Y_{NB}(X - 30)$, $0 \leq X \leq 45$, but it seems that it would break down in the next decade.

Exhibit 14 shows an absence of wealthy native born and foreign born above age 60. This is a contrast from 1860 where we found an extremely affluent older group born in the United States. The trend lines for the data are $W_{NB} = \$603(1.078)^X$ and $W_{FB} = \$672(1.041)^X$, $20 \leq$ age ≤ 69. Interestingly, $W_{NB}(X) = W_{FB}(X + 20)$ holds in the middle age group. This is contrasted with 1860 when there was a 30-year lag.

We are unable effectively to compare the average wealth of those age 40 in 1860 with that of those age 50 in 1870 except indirectly by using our relative accumulation rates. The 7.8 and 4.1 per cent apparent accumulation rates in 1870 may be compared to those of 8.3 and 6.6 per cent in 1860. Either the position of the young improved relative to the old, or the position of the old deteriorated relative to that of the young. One might guess it to be the former since the relative supply of the young was less in 1870 than in 1860. This large drop of the poor young was responsible for a 5 per cent decrease in the overall wealth concentration coefficient from 1860 to 1870.

D. WEALTH DISTRIBUTION IN WISCONSIN
IN 1850 AND 1870

The position of wealth in Wisconsin in 1850 and 1870 has been studied extensively in a fashion similar to that used for 1860. One should guard against presenting too much detail because of two defects. The 1850 values are only real estate values, while those for 1860 include an estimate of personal estate. Thus it is difficult to make 1850—1860 comparisons. The 1870 values fail to reflect any growth in real wealth per capita from 1860 to 1870 in Milwaukee and give only a 1.3 per cent per year increase in real wealth in the state.

Exhibit 14
Average Wealth[a] of Native-Born and Foreign-Born Males, Classified by Age for
Milwaukee County in 1870 and of Adult Males in Milwaukee County and Wisconsin
in 1870

Wealth in
dollars

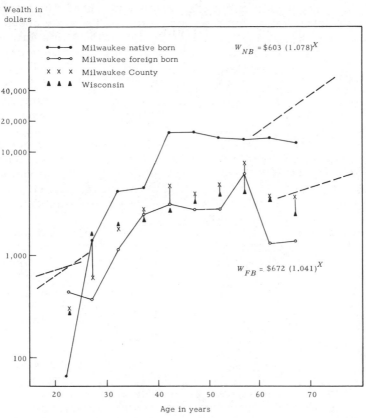

$W_{NB} = \$603 \ (1.078)^X$

$W_{FB} = \$672 \ (1.041)^X$

Age in years

[a]Wealth averages are for five-year intervals beginning at age 20. The 65–69
average wealth value has been replaced by the 65-and-up average.

Source: Schedule 1 of the 1870 Census.

However, there is strong merit in examining the 1850 data, since real
estate must have been at least 80 per cent of total estate at that stage.[2]
The relative dispersion in the 1870 values is of merit and can be compared to 1860 measures of relative inequality.

It is recalled from Chapter 3 that three procedures were employed:
a non-stratified sample of individuals, a sample stratified by size of
wealth and by county, and regression analyses of county data. These
three techniques were also utilized for both the 1850 and the 1870 data.
The results of these analyses will be discussed briefly. Table 15 has
some of the results of the non-stratified sample and Table 16 some results from the stratified samples. We see that the Gini coefficients
for all persons in 1850, 1860, and 1870 were 0.77, 0.75, and 0.74. By

Table 15. Frequency Distributions of Real Estate Values in 1850 and Real and Personal Estate Values in 1860 and 1870 for Males 20 and Older, Classified by Nativity and Occupation, Wisconsin

Dollar value of lower-class limit	All persons	Farmers		Non-farmers	
		Native born	Foreign born	Native born	Foreign born

(The ratio of the number of adult males in the cell in 1850 to the number of adult males in Wisconsin in 1850)

1850:					
0−	0.462	0.095	0.078	0.129	0.161
1−	.052	.007	.021	.008	.016
200−	.110	.030	.051	.014	.015
400−	.175	.073	.064	.020	.017
1,000−	.117	.060	.028	.021	.007
2,000−	.056	.034	.010	.008	.004
4,000−	.022	.009	.004	.006	.003
10,000−	.006	.003	.001	.003	.001
	1.000	0.310[a]	0.256[a]	0.211[a]	0.223[a]

(Median, arithmetic mean, and Gini coefficient in 1850)

Median	$150	$450	$200	$ 0	$ 0
$\bar{X}$	$626	$896	$556	$711	$252
$\bar{R}$	0.733	0.649	0.678	0.867	0.904

(The ratio of the number of adult males in the cell in 1860 to the number of adult males in Wisconsin in 1860)

1860:					
0−	0.288	0.070	0.080	0.054	0.085
1−	.103	.017	.024	.022	.040
200−	.086	.018	.023	.018	.026
400−	.166	.043	.064	.022	.037
1,000−	.160	.053	.067	.020	.020
2,000−	.114	.044	.041	.016	.012
4,000−	.065	.028	.018	.012	.008
10,000−	.019	.006	.002	.007	.004
	1.000[a]	0.279	0.319	0.171	0.232

(Median, arithmetic mean, and Gini coefficient in 1860)

Median	$ 350	$ 800	$ 600	$ 300	$115
$\bar{X}$	$1,486	$2,030	$1,199	$1,840	$964
$\bar{R}$	0.752	0.711	0.643	0.811	0.839

(The ratio of the number of adult males in the cell in 1870 to the number of adult males in Wisconsin in 1870)

1870:					
0−	0.356	0.067	0.069	0.085	0.135
1−	.025	.004	.006	.004	.011
200−	.041	.011	.009	.007	.015
400−	.119	.020	.040	.022	.037
1,000−	.138	.026	.059	.025	.028
2,000−	.149	.042	.067	.016	.024
4,000−	.132	.043	.062	.014	.013
10,000−	.040	.011	.010	.011	.007
	1.000	0.223[a]	0.322	0.184	0.271[a]

(Median, arithmetic mean, and Gini coefficient in 1870)

Median	$ 742	$1,349	$1,400	$ 275	$ 70
$\bar{X}$	$2,369	$2,649	$2,592	$3,018	$1,435
$\bar{R}$	0.741	0.647	0.600	0.861	0.844

[a]Figures in these columns do not add to totals because of rounding.

Source: These data are based on samples of males 20 and older of size 1,900 in 1850, 9542 in 1860, and 1663 in 1870, obtained by examining one line in each legible 40 in 1850, in each legible 20 in 1860, and in each legible 160 in 1870 of the census manuscripts. The samples thus account for 76,000 of the 84,479 adult males in 1850, 190,840 of 199,476 in 1860, and 266,080 of 263,900 in 1870.

Table 16. Frequency Distribution of Rich Males[a] 20 and Older,
          Classified by Real Estate Values in 1850, and
          Real and Personal Estate Values in 1860 and
          1870, Wisconsin

Real estate or wealth value	Number of persons		
(lower-class limit in dollars)	1850	1860	1870
0–	84,341	198,268	261,340
20,000–	115	783	1,732
40,000–	10	198	385
60,000–	2	95	166
80,000–	1	34	74
100,000–	10	86	203
	84,479	199,464	263,900
100,000–	7	61	162
200,000–	2	14	31
300,000–	1	7	3
400,000		1	2
500,000		3	5
	10	86	203

[a]These data are complete enumerations of declarations of $20,000
and more. The number below this level is obtained by using the residual from the size of the adult male population. The consumer price
index, C, in 1850, 1860, and 1870 was 0.90, 1.00, and 1.41. The index of adult male population, P, was 0.423, 1.000, 1.317. C times P
is 0.38, 1.00, and 1.86. Thus the 86 persons above $100,000 in 1860
would be the equivalent of 86 times 1.86, or 160 persons in 1870 without considering productivity increases.

Source: Census manuscripts.

1850 there were already a few individuals holding a large share of
wealth since 10 men reporting over $100,000 had 3.5 per cent of the
total real estate. The 86 men above $100,000 in 1860 had 5.3 per cent
of 1860 wealth, and the 203 above $100,000 in 1870 had 5.8 per cent of
1870 wealth. Our list of 10 in 1850 shows:

Real estate value	Age	Occupation	County in Wisconsin	Place of birth
$300,000	30	Blacksmith	Kenosha	Germany
225,000	36	Landowner	Milwaukee	Maryland
220,000	47	Merchant	Kenosha	New York
150,000	54	Landowner	Milwaukee	New York
150,000	48	Manufacturer	Kenosha	Massachusetts
150,000	36	Lawyer	Rock	New York
142,000	54	None	Milwaukee	New York
110,000	46	Merchant	Milwaukee	New York
105,000	34	Merchant	Milwaukee	New York
100,000	30	Banker	Milwaukee	New York

Nine of the 10 were native born; the median age was 41; 6 were from
Milwaukee and 3 from Kenosha. Four of the 6 from Milwaukee appeared
on the list for 1860 in Chapter 2. Their aggregate real estate value
had increased from $622,000 in 1850 to $1,620,000 in 1860. The 203
men listed in Table 16 for 1870 were of a different character. Of these,
86 were from Milwaukee, as contrasted with 46 in 1860. Prominent besides Alexander Mitchell at $1,832,000, were a leather manufacturer
and distiller from Milwaukee reporting $900,000 and $550,000, respectively, the president of a telegraph company from Kenosha reporting
$670,000, a lumberman from La Crosse at $650,000, and a threshing
machine manufacturer from Racine at $430,000. The industrial revolu-
tion demonstrated its effects in the 1870 data.

It is important to note that only a little more than half of adult males
were property owners in 1850. There were a number of laws which gov-
erned the distribution of land ownership in Wisconsin, both before and
after it became a state. Prior to statehood, three acts were of crucial
significance. The first of these was an act passed in 1807 which prohibited pre-emption; though nominally in force until 1832, it was
widely ignored, especially in burgeoning territories like Wisconsin.
The second was an 1820 act, which prohibited sale of public lands on
credit, set the minimum price at $1.25 an acre, and the minimum tract
at 80 acres. During the 1830's, a number of statutes allowing limited
pre-emption rights were passed, repealed, repassed with amendments,
etc. Their provisions were generally the same—right to pre-empt
quarter sections by settlers who occupied and farmed them, sales at
regularly scheduled times, settlers who could precede surveyors. These
principles were finally realized completely in what was the third major
piece of legislation affecting Wisconsin, the 1841 "Log Cabin Bill,"
or "Permanent Prospective Preemption Law."[3]

The right of preemption was open to the head of a family, to a man over twenty-one years
of age, to a widow—these to be citizens of the United States—or to aliens who had declared their intention of becoming such. The applicant was required to swear that he had
not to exceed [i.e., did not own more than] 320 acres of land other than his preemption
claim. To such a person the preemption act gave the right to settle on a piece of land,
160 acres in extent, and at a subsequent date to buy the same free from competitive bids,
at the minimum government price.[4]

That is to say, to purchase some land, the settler had to be finan-
cially able to bring his family west, erect some sort of house to see
them through a Wisconsin winter, have tools and seeds adequate to
farm his plot through one growing season, meanwhile purchasing food
to keep his family alive, and at length to come up with as much as
$200 cash to purchase the land outright from the government. As all
sorts of people never tired of pointing out during the ante-bellum period,
this was a remarkably restrictive land distribution policy.

It became slightly more restrictive two years after its passage by
the addition of clauses limiting the right of pre-emption to those men

who did not own land elsewhere in a territory where they wished to
file such a claim, and who had never filed a claim in any other state
or territory. Furthermore, its limitation of the use of pre-emption
claims to land already surveyed made it still more difficult for the
average poor man to use the law to his advantage.

In 1853 and 1854 bills were passed allowing the pre-emption right
to precede surveying. In 1862 there was passed another land law which
had the potential materially to affect the distribution of land in Wisconsin. This was the Homestead Act, which provided that settlers
could acquire free (except for a minimal filing charge) farms of up to
160 acres simply by living on them for five consecutive years. There
were amendments and alterations to this, but no significant ones before 1870. Here, at last, was the start of a policy genuinely designed
to put land into the hands of the landless. The startling fact is that it
had little effect on the distribution of wealth in Wisconsin. Perhaps
the margin of land it might apply to in Wisconsin was not large.

Were the 40,000 in Wisconsin without land in 1850 to buy it in a
few years and join the 44,000 with land? Perhaps the population of
adult males was no larger than 44,000 four years earlier than 1850.
This leads to the question of how much time elapsed between making
a claim and actual purchase of the land. I have not been able to obtain an exact answer. There were 6,441 pre-emption declarations
made in the Milwaukee land district in the six-year period from 1841
to October, 1847, but by the latter date only 40 had been paid.[5] At
least some of the 40,000 men without wealth in our table might soon
purchase their land but had not as of the census date. There is a
further problem in that the number 44,000 with wealth in real estate is
substantially larger than the 20,177 farms reported in the census in
1850. We shall see, furthermore, that in one sense manufacturing, in
the forms of lumbering and mining, was relatively more important at
the frontier. The least inequality one might assert as existing in 1850
was that among the 44,000 with wealth, who had a Gini R of 0.58. The
maximum bound is perhaps the 0.77 given in Table 15 from the non-
stratified sample or the 0.79 from the stratified sample. The 0.77 is
probably the better measurement. It includes the tremendous element
of landless manpower coming into the area in the short run. Surely one
must include this element since it was a continuing phenomenon as
long as immigration and migration were important.

Let us now examine the columns for all persons in Table 15. Gini
R's (R: 0.77, 0.75, 0.74) for 1850, 1860, and 1870 means there was
no change in overall inequality in the 20-year period. This is a very
remarkable finding, considering the dramatic changes in the factors
determining wealth. The increase in number of wealthy was counter-
balanced by a sizable increase in the median wealth value and a constant per cent of persons below $200 wealth, at least from 1860 to
1870. Assuming estate values in 1850 would have been 25 per cent
larger if personal estate had been included, and considering that

prices were 10 per cent higher in 1860 than 1850 and 41 per cent higher
in 1870 than 1860,

| | Average annual per cent of change in real wealth per adult male | |
	Median	Mean
1850–1860	5.3	5.5
1860–1870	4.2	1.3
1850–1870	4.8	3.4

There is evidence of substantial betterment of middle groups during
this period.

Turning to occupational and nativity classifications, we note that
the three samples show an increase in the per cent farmers (F: 0.57,
0.60, 0.54) in the first ten years but a drop for the two decades. The
per cent foreign born (FB: 0.48, 0.55, 0.59) increased significantly for
the period. Table 17 highlights the aging of the population. Those in
the age group 20–29 decreased from 37 to 31 to 29 per cent, while the
median age of males 20 and older increased from 35.6 to 37.6 to 39.9.
Thus from 1860 to 1870, the increase in relative farm population would
be thought to lead to less inequality, the increase in the relative
foreign-born population to greater inequality, and the increase in average age to less inequality. The Gini R levels among farmers were
(R_F: 0.67, 0.69, 0.62) and among non-farmers were (R_{NF}: 0.89, 0.83,
0.86); among native born (R_{NB}: 0.75, 0.75, 0.76) and foreign born
(R_{FB}: 0.79, 0.83, 0.72). Inequality of the young was (age 20–29:
0.77, 0.83, 0.74). These lead to mixed results and it is perhaps advisable to trace specific groups for the two decades.

| | Gini R | | |
	Age 20–29 in 1850	Age 30–39 in 1860	Age 40–49 in 1870
All persons	0.823	0.710	0.621
Native Born	.813	.684	.596
Foreign Born	.820	.719	.635
Farmers	.707	.616	.536
Non-farmers	.921	.807	.717

For all persons age 30–39 in 1850, 40–49 in 1860, and 50–59 in 1870,
the Gini R changed from 0.75 to 0.65 to 0.66. One has the impression,
then, that it is the young in each generation producing greater inequality. This is particularly true for the young who were foreign born and
non-farmers.

Multiple regression equations for the various situations are:

$$\text{1850:} \quad \log RE = 0.5824 + 0.0258 \, age, \quad N = 1,900, \quad r^2 = 0.05,$$
$$(0.0026)$$
$$RE = \$3.82 \; (1.061)^{age}$$

Table 17. Number, Mean, and Concentration Coefficient of Real
Estate Values in 1850, and Real and Personal Estate
Values in 1870, Classified by Age, Nativity, and Sex,
Wisconsin

	Age			
Nativity-occupation	20 & up	20—29	30—39	40—49

	(The ratio of the number of adult males in the cell to the number of adult males in Wisconsin)			
1850:[a]				
All persons	1.000	0.372[b]	0.303	0.170
Native born	.521	.197	.149	.090
Foreign born	.479	.174	.154	.080
Farmers[c]	.566	.177	.167	.112
Non-farmers	.434	.195	.136	.058
1870:[d]				
All persons	1.000	.289	.235[b]	.209[b]
Native born	.406	.145	.090	.085
Foreign born	.594	.144	.144	.123
Farmers	.545	.130	.126	.116
Non-farmers	.455	.159	.109	.093

	(The arithmetic mean, in dollars)			
1850:[a]				
All persons	626	315	777	895
Native born	820	408	1,087	1,101
Foreign born	415	208	476	664
Farmers[c]	741	432	840	919
Non-farmers	476	208	700	849
1870:[d]				
All persons	2,369	976	2,100	3,001
Native born	2,815	1,350	2,654	3,277
Foreign born	2,063	598	1,753	2,810
Farmers	2,615	960	2,312	3,355
Non-farmers	2,074	988	1,855	2,558

	(The Gini coefficient, R)			
1850:[a]				
All persons	0.773	0.823	0.748	0.717
Native born	.746	.813	.708	.672
Foreign born	.786	.820	.765	.760
Farmers[c]	.670	.707	.633	.610
Non-farmers	.891	.921	.863	.872
1870:[d]				
All persons	.741	.895	.716	.621
Native born	.764	.919	.712	.596
Foreign born	.718	.837	.708	.635
Farmers	.620	.773	.617	.536
Non-farmers	.860	.957	.814	.717

[a]The sample size for this year is 1,900.
[b]Figures in these columns do not add to totals because of rounding.
[c]The term "farm laborer" was not used in the 1850 census; hence
there are fewer farmers recorded in that year than in others.
[d]The sample size for this year is 1,663.

Source: See sources to Table 15.

1860: log W = 0.8543 + 0.0325 age, N = 9,542, r^2 = 0.09,
                    (0.0011)

W = \$7.15(1.078)^{age}

1870: log W = 0.5161 + 0.0395 age, N = 1,663, r^2 = 0.12,
                    (0.0026)

W = \$3.28(1.096)^{age}

1850: log RE = 1.3642 + 0.0188 age - 0.9356 NF - 0.2587 FB,
                      (0.0025)   (0.0620)   (0.0605)

N = 1,900, r^2 = 0.16

1860: log W = 1.1558 + 0.0314 age - 0.2597 NF - 0.2067 FB,
                      (0.0010)   (0.0281)   (0.0275)

N = 9,542, r^2 = 0.09

1870: log W = 1.0412 + 0.0359 age - 0.7370 NF - 0.0803 FB,
                      (0.0026)   (0.0733)   (0.0740)

N = 1,663, r^2 = 0.17

1850: RE = \$23.10(1.044)^{age} (0.116)^{NF} (0.551)^{FB}

1860: W = \$14.32(1.075)^{age} (0.437)^{NF} (0.621)^{FB}

1870: W = \$11.00(1.086)^{age} (0.184)^{NF} (0.831)^{FB}.

These equations point first to a great deal of regularity for data covering a ten-year span. Secondly, they point out the fact that, for all
adult males in Wisconsin, age became increasingly important, and in
1870 farming reasserted itself as being important in the determination
of wealth.

It should not be inferred that the non-farm sector was not to become
the dynamic sector. The number of *farms* reported in the census as a
per cent of the number of adult males for Wisconsin was:

1850	23.8	1890	30.6
1860	34.4	1900	28.8
1870	37.6	1910	25.0
1880	37.8	1920	22.1

The number of farms per adult male reached its peak between 1870 and
1880, but the non-farm sector still deserves careful scrutiny. For the
non-farm group:

1850: log RE = 0.3536 + 0.0229 age - 0.3815 FB, N = 825,
           (0.0041)   (0.0908)

r^2 = 0.06, RE = \$2.26(1.054)^{age} (0.416)^{FB}

1860: log W = 0.8403 + 0.0320 age - 0.3216 FB, N = 3,838,
           (0.0018)   (0.0443)

r^2 = 0.09, W = \$6.92(1.076)^{age} (0.477)^{FB}

1870: log W = 0.3688 + 0.0381 age - 0.3220 FB, N = 756,
           (0.0042)   (0.1145)

r^2 = 0.10, W = \$2.34(1.092)^{age} (0.476)^{FB}.

Native born continued to assert an economic advantage throughout the
period with wealth 2 to 2.5 times that of foreign born. The analysis at
this point is far from complete because many non-farmers were living
in essentially rural areas. We return to our study of counties as the
microcomponents so that we may investigate the very important variable, density.

E. A COUNTY ANALYSIS USING INDEXES
OF ECONOMIC DEVELOPMENT

Tables 18 and 19 give development indexes for the 31 Wisconsin
counties in 1850 and the 58 counties in 1870. Certain details will be
extracted from these and a similar table in Chapter 3 for 1860.

	Low density	Medium density	High density	All
	(The Gini R, with the number of counties in parentheses)			
1850	0.841 (10)	0.762 (10)	0.748 (11)	0.785 (31)
1860	.762 (12)	.681 (30)	.723 (14)	.709 (56)
1870	.778 (14)	.660 (32)	.697 (12)	.697 (58)

There is no difference in the 1860 and 1870 U-shaped patterns since
one should add about 0.03 to the 1870 figures to allow for 20-year-olds
not reported in the census. The high inequality persisted among the
sparsely populated counties and the lowest inequality persisted among
the medium group. The high density group could be further subdivided
to include the counties containing large cities. In 1870, Milwaukee
County had an R of 0.853, Racine County an R of 0.815. Counties sur-

rounding Milwaukee and Racine had low coefficients: Ozaukee had an R of 0.576, Walworth an R of 0.526, Jefferson an R of 0.652. Perhaps the urban areas provided better opportunities for the available farm and non-farm labor force alike.

We conclude with some multiple regression equations for the three census years. When the straight line in logarithms is used as the model, one actually finds that inequality was negatively related to density or urbanity by 1870, thus reasserting the position in 1850:

$$1850: \quad \log R = -0.0741 - 0.0362 \log D, \quad N = 31, \quad r^2 = -0.19$$
$$(0.0140)$$

$$1860: \quad \log R = -0.1403 - 0.0114 \log D, \quad N = 56, \quad r^2 = -0.02$$
$$(0.0110)$$

$$1870: \quad \log R = -0.1176 - 0.0361 \log D, \quad N = 58, \quad r^2 = -0.12.$$
$$(0.0129)$$

This negative relationship holds also for R and W:

$$1850: \quad \log R = 0.1464 - 0.0997 \log RE, \quad N = 31, \quad r^2 = -0.27$$
$$(0.0307)$$

$$1860: \quad \log R = -0.2909 + 0.0451 \log W, \quad N = 56, \quad r^2 = +0.02$$
$$(0.0414)$$

$$1870: \quad \log R = -0.0919 - 0.0785 \log W, \quad N = 58, \quad r^2 = -0.07$$
$$(0.0385)$$

$$1850-1860: \quad r^2(R_{W,1860}, \, R_{RE,1850}) = 0.29, \quad N = 31$$

$$1860-1870: \quad r^2(R_{W,1870}, \, R_{W,1860}) = 0.43, \quad N = 56.$$

These negative correlations are consistent with the idea of decreased inequality in the long run since both D and W would continue to increase.

In 1860, wealth and density were related strongly only after elimination of the dozen counties of lowest density:

$$1850: \quad \log RE = 2.2320 + 0.3631 \log D, \quad N = 31, \quad r^2 = 0.71$$
$$(0.0435)$$

$$1860: \quad \log W = 2.9680 + 0.0879 \log D, \quad N = 56, \quad r^2 = 0.11$$
$$(0.0340)$$

Table 18. Indexes of Development for Thirty-One Counties, Classified by
Population Density,[a] Wisconsin, 1850

Development index Z	Corre-lation coeffi-cient	Density, D = Number of persons per sq. mile			
		$D < 1.0$ (11 counties)	$1.0 < D \leq 2.0$ (10 counties)	$D > 2.0$ (10 counties)	All D (All 31 counties)
	$r(N = 31)$	(Arithmetic mean of the 11, 10, 10, and 31 values)			
Density, D, or persons per square mile in 1850	1.00	0.24	1.52	4.25	1.95
Arithmetic mean value of real estate per male 20 & up in 1850	0.84	$238	$453	$662	$442
Gini R of real estate values of males 20 & up in 1850	−0.43	0.841	0.762	0.748	0.785
Median age of males 20 & up in 1850	0.47[b]	29.6	33.6	33.9	32.2
Ratio of the number of foreign born to all persons in 1850	0.43[b]	0.252	0.331	0.361	0.313
Ratio of the number of hands employed in manufacturing to adult males in 1850	−0.45[b]	0.139	0.049	0.075	0.088
Ratio of number of farms to number of adult males in 1870	0.23[b]	0.175	0.209	0.277	0.219
Number of acres of improved land per farm in 1870	0.34	42	49	50	47
Cash value of farms per acre of improved and unimproved land in 1850	0.75	$5.40	$7.24	$11.87	$8.08
Ratio of the number of acres of improved farm land to improved plus unimproved farm land in 1850	0.60[b]	0.195	0.281	0.371	0.279
Per cent of adult males with a non-zero value for real estate in 1850	0.49[b]	35.4	46.1	50.9	43.9
Arithmetic mean value of adult males with non-zero real estate, 1850	0.42	$897	$989	$1,356	$1,075
Gini R of non-zero values for real estate in 1850	0.04	0.536	0.533	0.519	0.530
Average monthly wage to a farm hand in 1850	−0.83	$18.00	$12.60	$11.00	$14.00
Average to a daylaborer without board in 1850	−0.57	$1.14	$0.94	$0.91	$1.00
Average to a carpenter without board in 1850	−0.50	$1.77	$1.53	$1.45	$1.59
Arithmetic mean value of real estate per male 20 & up in 1860	0.41	$815	$1,013	$1,317	$1,041
Average of real plus personal wealth per male 20 & up in 1860	0.40	$1,084	$1,557	$1,730	$1,445
Gini R of real plus personal wealth of males 20 & up in 1860	−0.00	0.719	0.699	0.739	0.719

[a]Each county has been given an equal weight in the computation of averages.
[b]From $Z = a + b \log D$. Others are from $\log Z = C + d \log D$.

Source: Manuscript analyses of the 1850 census, in the possession of the author.

Table 19. Indexes of Development for Fifty-Eight Counties, Classified by
Population Density,[a] Wisconsin, 1870

Development Index Z	Corre- lation coeffi- cient	Density, D = Number of persons per sq. mile			
		$D < 10$ (14 counties)	$10 < D < 50$ (32 counties)	$D > 50$ (12 counties)	All D (All 58 counties)
	$r(N = 58)$	(Arithmetic mean of the 14, 32, 12 and 58)			
Density, D, or persons per square mile in 1870	1.00	3.8	27.0	88.4	34.1
Arithmetic mean value of wealth per male 21 & up in 1870	0.73	$1,114	$1,619	$2,685	$1,717
Gini R of wealth values of males 21 & up in 1870	−0.35	0.778	0.661	0.697	0.687
Ratio of number of males 21 & up to total number of persons in 1870	−0.74[b]	0.304	0.241	0.239	0.256
Ratio of number of foreign-born to total number of persons in 1870	−0.03[b]	0.373	0.316	0.386	0.344
Ratio of the number of hands employed in manufacturing to the number of adult males in 1870	−0.08[b]	0.182	0.122	0.193	0.151
Ratio of number of farms to number of adult males in 1870	0.42[b]	0.244	0.456	0.477	0.398
Number of acres of improved land per farm in 1870	0.54	32	52	62	49
Cash value of farms per acre of improved and unimproved farm land in 1870	0.38	$10.92[c]	$18.21	$50.68	$21.56[c]
Ratio of number of acres of improved to improved plus unimproved farm land in 1870	0.48[b]	0.277	0.413	0.669	0.433
Gini R of farm acreage including an estimate of landless adult males ($= R_{land}$) in 1870	−0.44	0.833	0.708	0.739	0.745
Number of paupers in 1870	0.58	10	21	64	27
Average annual cost of labor per employee in manufacturing in 1870	−0.13	$295	$261	$262	$269
Average monthly wage to a farm hand in 1870	−0.70	$24	$19	$16	$19
Average to a daylaborer without board in 1870	−0.50	$1.85	$1.57	$1.58	$1.64

(continued)

Table 19 (continued)

Development Index Z	Corre-lation coeffi-cient	Density, D = Number of persons per sq. mile			
		$D < 10$ (14 counties)	$10 < D < 50$ (32 counties)	$D > 50$ (12 counties)	All D (All 58 counties)
Average to a carpenter without board in 1870	−0.47	$3.14	$2.59	$2.58	$2.72
Ratio of assessed personal estate to assessed personal and real estate in 1870	0.39[b]	0.16	0.27	0.22	0.23
Ratio of VEOI to VEOT in 1870	−0.05[b/d]	0.44	0.46	0.50	0.46
VEOI per male 21 & up in 1870	0.01	$2,792	$2,150	$2,803	$2,440
Gini R of wealth values of males 20 & up in 1860	−0.11	0.744	0.688	0.724	0.709
Arithmetic mean value of wealth per male 20 & up in 1860	0.41	$968	$1,205	$1,507	$1,210

[a]Each county has been given an equal weight in the computation of averages.
[b]From $Z = a + b \log D$. Others are from $\log Z = c + d \log D$.
[c]Does not include Bayfield at $99.00 and Douglas at $71.93.
[d]There are some extreme values.

Source: Manuscript analyses of the 1870 census, in the possession of the author.

1860: $\log W = 2.8136 + 0.2023 \log D$, $N = 44$, $r^2 = 0.25$
(0.0538)

1870: $\log W = 2.9190 + 0.2552 \log D$, $N = 58$, $r^2 = 0.53$
(0.0317)

1850−1860: $r^2(W_{1860}, RE_{1850}) = 0.23$

1860−1870: $r^2(W_{1870}, W_{1860}) = 0.43$.

In 1850 and again in 1870, the relationship was very high even including all counties. Employing the implications from population growth with our density functions gives:

1850: $RE = \$171(1.086)^t$ if $D = (1.258)^t$ as from 1850 to 1860

1860: $W = \$661(1.020)^t$ for $N = 44$ if $D = (1.097)^t$ as from 1850 to 1860

1870: $W = \$830(1.030)^t$ if $D = (1.125)^t$ as from 1840 to 1870

1870: $W = \$30(1.016)^t$ if $D = (1.064)^t$ as from 1850 to 1870.

The very early years have an implicit per capita growth of more than 8 per cent a year. Later per capita growth approaches 2 per cent a year.

From the standpoint of income distribution, we are interested in wage rates for day laborers:

1850: $\log Y_{DL} = 0.3288 - 0.1307 \log RE$, $N = 31$, $r^2 = -0.33$
                            (0.0348)

1860: $\log Y_{DL} = 0.6833 - 0.2191 \log W$, $N = 32$, $r^2 = -0.18$
                            (0.0859)

1870: $\log Y_{DL} = 0.5821 - 0.1157 \log W$, $N = 58$, $r^2 = -0.13$.
                            (0.0398)

There is an indication that wage rates and wealth averages were not so strongly related in a negative direction by 1870. It would be interesting to know in what year after 1870 the direction became positive; at that point income inequality would perhaps be less in the more urban areas than in the rural areas.

The period from 1850 to 1870 has been studied in Milwaukee and in Wisconsin. The wealth inequality level in Wisconsin remained relatively the same throughout the period with middle groups doing well compared to the young, who were often foreign-born non-farmers. Sparsely populated frontier areas had large inequality while counties near urban areas seemed to have less. Milwaukee had large inequality in 1850 and 1860 but had a 5 per cent decrease from 1860 to 1870. By 1870, there was an inverse relationship among the counties between inequality and population density and between inequality and per capita wealth.

Chapter 5

Wealth and Income Distributions of Nationality Groups

If the exact determinants of the wealth of foreign-born persons could be discovered, a great deal of progress could be made in the understanding of the motives of the immigrants and their movements in the United States. It is possible to focus on one or two nationality groups in ascertaining differences between the United States and other countries. Emphasis will be placed primarily on Norwegians because of the availability of distribution data pertaining to them.

A. INCOME AND WEALTH IN KRISTIANSAND, NORWAY, 1865

An important port of emigration to the United States from Norway was Kristiansand on the southern coast. It was a city of 9,500 in 1855 and is located in the county of Vest-Agder, which was estimated in 1910 to have lost half its potential labor force to emigration. Excellent income and wealth data exist for the last half of the nineteenth century in the city, and the year 1865 is chosen as an appropriate point for comparison because there was a census in that year.[1]

Exhibit 15 shows the wealth and income distributions in Milwaukee County,[2] stemming largely from persons living in the city of Milwaukee, and in the city of Kristiansand. The *speciedaler* was the Norwegian monetary unit, having approximately the value of an American dollar: in much of the literature and in letters by persons who wrote home from America there was no distinction made between the two.[3] In 1865 the exchange rate was 4.60 *riksdaler* to a pound sterling, which then had a dollar value of $4.87; thus the equivalent of one *riksdaler*[4] was $0.934. (It is understood that exchange rates may not adequately reflect consumer living costs.)

The wealth distributions indicate that the wealth held by the very rich was approximately the same in both cities, but that levels were

Exhibit 15
Wealth and Income Distribution in Milwaukee County and in Kristiansand,
Norway, in 1860, 1864, and 1865

X = wealth or income in
dollars or *specie dalers*

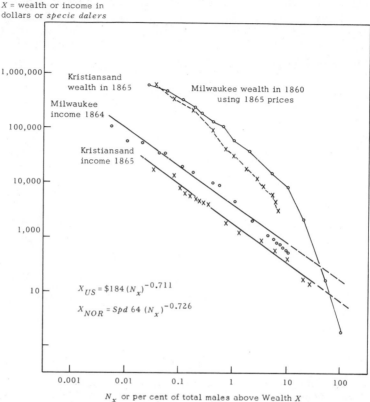

N_x or per cent of total males above Wealth X

Sources: Kristiansand figures, *Ligningsprotokoller* (official assessment records in
the Norwegian *Statsarkiver*); Milwaukee wealth figures, Schedule 1 of the 1860
Census; Milwaukee income figures, income tax declarations (see Chapters 1 and 7).

not sustained for the middle group in the case of Kristiansand. The
92nd wealth percentile in Milwaukee was 4 times that in Kristiansand.
One is led to believe that this period in Kristiansand was still dominated by a few individual merchants and ship-owners while Milwaukee
County offered a wider base of opportunity for a middle-class or middle-
rung group.

Comparison of income distributions in the two cities reveals interesting results. The evidence indicates that there was probably little
difference in relative dispersion of upper income groups between the
two. Least-squares results are, for Milwaukee: n = 18, $0.000055 \leq$
$N_X \leq 0.103$; $\log X = 2.2650 - 0.7109 \log N_X$, where X is 1864 income
in current dollars; and for Kristiansand: n = 23, $0.000354 \leq N_X \leq$
0.254; $\log X = 1.8063 - 0.7255 \log N_X$, where X is 1865 income in
current *speciedaler*. Unfortunately, there are no data for the lower

portions of the distribution for either city and one is forced to rely on
data for the upper portions as stated above.

It is noted that the slope, b, of the Milwaukee and Kristiansand
curves is almost the same. The implied concentration coefficient
$R = b/(2 - b)$ is thus similar for the two, being 0.55 in the case of
Milwaukee and 0.57 in the case of Kristiansand. Since the wealth-
income ratio for Milwaukee County is somewhat constant while that
for Kristiansand is not, there is evidence that the top wealth in Kristiansand may not have been so productive.

The implied lower limit of the equations, obtained by letting N_X =
1.00, is $184 for Milwaukee and $64 (*spd*) in the case of Kristiansand.
The ratio 64/184 is 29 per cent. The inference is that incomes were
three to three and one-half times as high in Milwaukee as in Kristiansand. This ratio is perhaps not far from what it is today in the two
cities: average male income in Kristiansand in 1950 was 8,100 *kroner*;
in Milwaukee in 1949 it was $3,280, which, at 7 *kroner* to a dollar,
gives a ratio of 35 per cent. The median daily wage rate in 1860 in
Milwaukee for a day laborer was $0.75; urban wage rates in Norway
for day laborers were $0.36. In 1850, the reported daily rate was $0.75
in Milwaukee and $0.25 in Norwegian areas. In 1870, the two rates
were $1.00 and $0.39.[5]

Perhaps even more important than the disparity in the income ratio
was the prevalence of relatively full employment in the United States.
Surely availability of land in the West was important. An immigrant
song quoted by Theodore Blegen reads:

I do not expect to find gold more easily there than elsewhere. No, I am ready to
work in the sweat of my brow. Through effort and industry I shall make for myself a new
home. 'You can make a home for yourself,' say many. 'Work and save here, where you
are, and then you can avoid going there to take a chance in the lottery of luck, to become a foreign slave.'

'My dear friend, do not talk this way. I have already tried; through my best years
I have labored here; but I am as far from my goal as when I first began, when I viewed
so hopefully the prospect of a home.'

'Nor does this mean slavery—for America is free. Work is not slavery; and thrift
is no lottery. In the free land of the West every man is a free-born citizen.'[6]

B. WEALTH DISTRIBUTION OF WISCONSIN

One difficulty with the comparison in Exhibit 15 is that a Norwegian
was nearly certain to have wealth and income well below the average
of that in the United States. An attempt was made to obtain wealth
data of Norwegians in Wisconsin by sampling four counties. Census
data for 1870 suggested that Dane County would have the most Norwegians. La Crosse County was chosen to represent several southern
and western counties. Racine and Waupaca counties were selected to
represent other areas. Distributions are given in Table 20.

Table 20. Distribution of Wealth Among Norwegians in Each of Four
Counties, Wisconsin, 1860

Lower-class limit in dollars	Dane County	La Crosse County	Waupaca County	Racine County	Total
20,000—	0	1	0	0	1
10,000—	2	0	0	0	2
8,000—	1	0	0	0	1
4,000—	25	0	0	4	29
2,000—	85	10	9	13	117
1,000—	129	35	26	11	201
800—	24	11	2	3	40
400—	42	11	20	4	77
200—	41	1	18	7	67
100—	85	1	4	6	96
80—	4	1	2	0	7
40—	46	0	4	3	53
20—	7	0	0	0	7
0—	170	66	18	28	282
	661	137	103	79	980[a]
$\bar{X}$	$976	$866	$756	$1,013	$941
R	0.662	0.696	0.525	0.669	0.665

(The number of Norwegian males 20 and up as a per cent
of the number of all males 20 and up)

	5.8	3.9	4.6	1.4	4.3

(The arithmetic mean for adult Norwegian males as a
per cent of that for all adult males)

	57.2	74.5	68.1	53.9	58.7

[a]The 980 cases are for males 20 and up, and were obtained by examining every second page of Schedule 1. The total number of Norwegians in
the state in 1860 was 21,442.

Source: Schedule 1 of the 1860 Census; U.S. Census Office. 8th Census, 1860. *Population of the United States in 1860* (GPO: Washington,
D.C., 1864), Table 1; U.S. Census Office. 8th Census, 1860. *Statistics
of the United States (Including Mortality, Property &c.,) in 1860* (GPO:
Washington, D.C., 1866), Table 3.

The information of Table 20 shows that average wealth of Norwegians
was about $900, or 60 per cent of the overall average. A sizeable num-
ber of cases had little or no wealth. This phenomenon may be attributed
in part to: transients stopping in various Norwegian centers located on
the Western routes; farmers who obtained land in very unproductive
areas; farm laborers, some of whom would never own land; sons living
on farms who in the future might obtain title to their fathers' farms; and
those who were non-farmers, some day laborers, some artisans. These

low-wealth groups are of extreme importance to an understanding of
the inequality of the period and should be described in some detail.

Transiency was very prevalent in our 4 counties. A count of all
males in them who had been born in Norway showed that of the 119 in
the age class 5–9, only 17 had attended school within the year. Of
the 118 in age class 10–14, only 22 had attended. For males, the ratio
of those under 20 years of age to those 20 and older was 0.60; among
all persons in the four counties, this ratio was 1.02 or, excluding those
age 0–5, was 0.68. According to Theodore Blegen, both Dane and La
Crosse counties were on the regular migration routes used by groups
of Norwegians who eventually settled in Fillmore County, Minnesota.[7]
Transients with low wealth should, therefore, be found in those counties.

It is instructive to examine first an endpoint of migration in Fillmore County, the township of Norway. This township had 160 males
20 years old and over, all but 1 born in Norway. Each listed occupation was farmer, farm hand, or farm laborer. Some of the 20 individuals
reporting no wealth had no stated occupation but each was living with
a farm family. Of those 20 persons with no wealth, 11 had the same
last name as the farmer who was head of the household and are assumed to be the sons of the head. Significantly, only 9 individuals
might have been considered to be farm hands.

In many ways, the census records of the township of Norway in
1860 are a quantification of the American dream of egalitarianism. Distribution data show:

(Lower limit of wealth class—frequency)

$	0 – 20	$1,200 –	23
	1 – 5	1,400 –	24
200 –	1	1,600 –	10
400 –	5	1,800 –	6
600 –	9	2,000 –	4
800 –	20	2,500 –	8
$1,000 –	23	3,000 –	2
			160

$\overline{X}$ = $1,158 R = 0.339.

The coefficient of 0.339 is remarkably small for wealth. It certainly
would be considered small for an income distribution in 1960. The
median age of the 160 was 35 years, with an even distribution between
ages 20 and 45. The arithmetic mean of wealth of $1,158 was similar
to the foreign-born wealth average of 35-year-olds in Milwaukee in
1860. A systematic sample of every tenth male yields the following
details:

Age	Wealth	Wife	Children born in Norway	Children born in U.S.	Age of oldest child born in U.S.
32	$ 750	Yes	2	2	4 yrs.
45	1,850	Yes	6	3	3 yrs.
20	(Son of a farmer with $1,450 and 6 children)				
28	1,200	Yes		2	4 yrs.
40	1,150	Yes	4	—	
30	2,750	Yes	3	2	4 yrs.
25	(Farm hand unattached living with a family of 8)				
23	(Farm hand unattached living with a family of 5)				
22	(Son of a farmer with $1,800 and 6 children)				
28	590	Yes	1	—	
20	(Farm hand, perhaps a relative of a family of 5)				
24	950	Yes	—	—	
30	1,100	Yes	2	1	3 yrs.
30	1,000	Yes	4	—	
42	1,500	Yes	7	1	2 yrs.
38	1,200	Yes	3	2	6 yrs.
28	1,400	Yes	3	2	3 yrs.

This was largely a group of young farmers with large families and very homogeneous resources: 75 per cent of the 160 had wealth above $800; of the remaining 40 males, 11 were sons of this group. The farm hand class was less than 10 per cent of the total.

Norway township of Fillmore County was the exception. Let us look at what might be the other end of the continuum, the township of Barre in central La Crosse County. There were 46 males 20 or older of Norwegian birth in the township in 1860.

(Lower limit of wealth class—frequency)

$ 0 –	24	$1,400 –	3
200 –	2	1,600 –	0
400 –	2	1,800 –	1
600 –	2	2,000 –	0
800 –	1	2,500 –	0
1,000 –	4	3,000 –	2
1,200 –	2		46

$\bar{X} = \$823$ $R = 0.700$

The concentration coefficient is more than twice as large as that in Norway township. The median was zero dollars, since 24 of the 46 reported no wealth. Only 1 of the 24 cases qualified as a son of a farmer. The rest had the vague title "laborer" or "farmer," except for a few where no occupation was stated. Yet the area was a farming region. Only 1 of the 46 had an occupation that might suggest otherwise: "mechanic."

A systematic sample of 1 in 10 yields 4 persons with the following information: a 30-year-old laborer, apparently single with no wealth; a 25-year-old farmer with a wife and a one-year-old son, no wealth; a 30-year-old laborer who was unattached and living with an unattached brother, no wealth; a 30-year-old farmer with a wife, one child born in Norway, two born in Wisconsin, $350 wealth. One has the impression that economic conditions were not satisfactory in the township. There may have been an excess of laborers. In any case, there were not many individuals who owned farms.

Let us describe only briefly our third example, the township of Scandinavia in Waupaca County. The distribution is essentially that given for Waupaca County in Table 20, with its mean of $756 and R of 0.525. In this case, the inequality coefficient is not large but neither is the mean. There seems to have been a sizeable group of farmers with real estate values under $800. In addition, approximately 10 per cent of the Norwegians had occupational titles other than "farmer" or "laborer." Many were located in the small village of the township. Examples with wealth are: carpenter, $100; postmaster, $800; tailor, $250; blacksmith, $350; clerk in store, $73; and shoemaker, $250.

The descriptions of the three townships lead to an understanding of the heterogeneity of economic holdings of Norwegians. One can now return to the comparison of Norwegians in Wisconsin with Norwegians in Norway. An attempt has been made to present Norwegian Pareto Curves for those living in Norway and Wisconsin on the same chart, Exhibit 16. The Kristiansand curve intersects the four-county curve approximately at an Nx of 0.08. The top 8 per cent of wealthholders in Kristiansand thus had substantially more wealth than their counterparts in Wisconsin. Below this level, the four-county curve shows strong wealth and presumably the majority of the lower 90 per cent in the four counties enjoyed greater material holdings than the same group in Norway.

The curves even give evidence that, below the 80th percentile, the average Norwegian in Wisconsin had more than the average person in Milwaukee. This statement is made subject to the confounding effects of age. The best that can be done is to examine a specific age class, such as that of 40-year-olds. An extended study of this age group was made in all counties in Wisconsin and it will be discussed in detail below. It suffices here to state that the curve for 40-year-old Norwegians was similar to that for Norwegians 20 years old or over in the four counties. This comparison is made in Exhibit 16 with slightly less inequality appearing in the 40-year-old curve. One is left with the impression that only the well-to-do group in Norway could match in wealthholding their counterparts among all males in Wisconsin and exceed their fellow countrymen who had emigrated. Below this wealth level the advantage clearly lay in Wisconsin, even among Norwegians.

Exhibit 16
Pareto Curves of Norwegian Wealth Distributions in Norway in 1865[a] and in
Four Wisconsin Counties in 1860

X or wealth in 1860
dollars or *specie dalers*

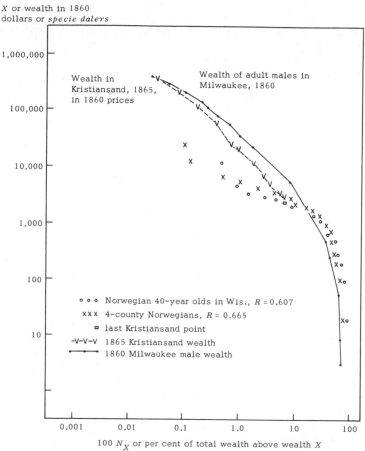

[a]The Kristiansand data have been deflated by the U.S. price index.

Sources: Kristiansand figures, *Ligningsprotokoller*; Milwaukee figures, Schedule
1 of the 1860 Census.

A dialect poem from the area of Telemark probably gives a much more
adequate expression than any quantitative formulation.

I am not going to stay in Norway any longer. I am going to America; that's the best
thing for me to do. I have heard that men who know how to use their hands can live well
there. Land is cheap, and heavy taxes don't eat up everything a farmer makes.

You hear in this country a lot of fine talk about liberty and equality and that the people hold the purse-strings; but the bureaucrats are paid too well, while the common people must struggle along.

A reply: 'I'll admit that in some things you are right; but I remember that there are many things in this world that might be mended. Many burdens have been lightened since Norway gained her independence, many abuses corrected, and many more will be. Suppose I can live in *Wisconsin* free from care and anxiety, what good is that if I am not happy there, but long every hour for home? Those who find life in Norway so full of hardships may perhaps discover that life in America is not so much more easy than in the country they left.[8]

An analysis of the 980 cases in the Norwegian study was made from the standpoint of age. One can say that, in general, the Milwaukee age-nativity model is appropriate for Norwegians in the four counties, both with respect to numbers and to average wealth. By five-year intervals we have

Age	20−24	25−29	30−34	35−39	40−44	45−49
Number	140	159	160	136	141	63
$\overline{X}$	280	680	1,030	950	1,340	1,240

Age	50−54	55−59	60−64	65−69	70−74	75−82
Number	78	40	35	15	9	4
$\overline{X}$	1,200	1,700	1,170	1,310	830	390

Age	20−82
Number	980
$\overline{X}$	940

The frequency distribution has a pattern similar to that of Milwaukee, with the modal class being from 30 to 34 years. The least-squares line fitted to frequency data from age 20 to 64 is $Y = 726\,(0.953)^A$, where A is the age in years and Y is the frequency per five-year interval. The apparent Norwegian population growth was 4.7 per cent per annum.
Average wealth figures given in Exhibit 17 are not so clear-cut. The scatter has essentially a shape ⌒. It will be recalled that in the Milwaukee presentation it was argued that the data for those older than age 60 or 70 were not appropriate to American experience; these persons may have come with their children. Certainly the number of persons involved drops radically from that prior to age 60 or 70. In any case, about the most favorable apparent growth rate is that between age 20 and 60. The equation here is $W = \$170\,(1.040)^A$, where W is the average wealth of a five-year class and A is the age in years. An average Norwegian in the four counties thus had an apparent rate of accumulation of 4 per cent a year; this is less than the 6 per cent rate found for foreign born in Milwaukee. It is interesting to note that the growth rate of wealth is less than that of population. The Norwegian group was thus not holding its own as a contributor to per capita growth in the four counties reflected in the 1860 data.

Exhibit 17
Average Wealth of Adult Norwegian Males for Four Counties in Wisconsin in 1860,
Classified by Age

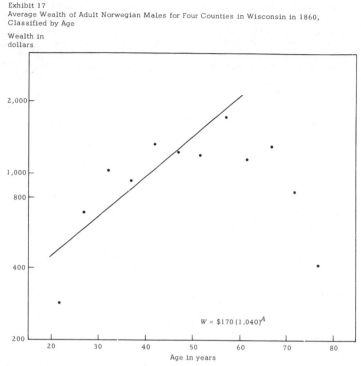

Source: Schedule 1 of the 1860 Census.

A further classification of the 980 Norwegians was made using the
simple dichotomy of farmer and non-farmer.

	Number	$\bar{X}$	R
Farmer	612	1,500	0.544
Non-farmer	368	180	.792
All	980	940	.665

The farmer group may be considered to be the substantial homogeneous
class constituting the success story among Norwegians. The other
group included laborers, carpenters, some sons of farmers, and probably some transients. Half of the 368 in this group reported no wealth.

C. DISTRIBUTIONS IN DENMARK IN 1870

Data for only one Norwegian city have been offered up to this point,
but a study of eight Norwegian cities has been made indicating that
figures for Kristiansand are representative of the general economic
growth during the industrial revolution.[9] Aside from the Norwegian

distributions, virtually the only additional evidence for European countries is some figures for Denmark, Prussia, and England.

A study was made of Danish income distributions in 1870. Only values at $A_X = 0.25$ and $A_X = 0.50$ are available, where $100\ A_X$ is the per cent of total income above X. The data in Table 21 show varying results that can be compared to our previous data. It will be recalled that for income data:

	Slope of inverse Pareto curve	Implied concentration coefficient
Milwaukee	0.711	0.55
Kristiansand	0.726	0.57

These data fall midway between those for provincial towns in Denmark and those for the entire country. Only the major cities of Denmark showed extreme inequality. The implied lower limits for the Danish data were $35 in the major cities and twice this level in the country.[10]

The only other data available prior to 1870 are income distributions for the top 3.6 per cent of the population in England in 1801 and 35.4

Table 21. Inequality of Income Among Persons, Classified by
       Urbanity, Denmark, 1870

A_X or per cent of income above X	L_X or number of persons above X	X in kroner[a]	Slope, b, of inverse Pareto curve	Implied R	Implied lower limit in kroner
Major cities of Copenhagen and Frederiksberg					
25	1,600	6,000	0.83	0.71	129
50	10,600	1,250			
100	105,684				
Provincial towns					
25	2,950	3,200	0.75	0.60	103
50	13,882	1,000			
100	111,144				
Farm districts					
25	12,700	2,400	0.59	0.42	271
50	47,700	1,100			
100	514,596				
Entire country					
25	14,700	3,200	0.67	0.50	223
50	72,100	1,100			
100	779,124				

[a]At the rate of exchange then current, one *krone* was worth about $0.27.

Source: Jens Warming, *Nationalokonomisk Tidskrift* (Copenhagen, 1907), XLV, p. 402.

per cent of the population in Prussia in 1854.[11] The distribution for
Prussia was reportedly quite equal (with an implied R of 0.38 and implied lower limit of 123 *marks*, or \$6 per person). That for England
had an implied R of 0.692.

D. WEALTH DISTRIBUTIONS OF OTHER NATIONALITY GROUPS IN WISCONSIN

Some notion of 1860 wealth levels for different nationality groups
living in Wisconsin may be informative. It is difficult to design a
sample large enough to encompass the important age variable and yet
preserve detail of nativity; 40-year-olds were singled out for special
study in an attempt to avoid a confounding effect from age. This group
reporting age as 40 includes some males whose real ages were in the
thirties and many whose real ages were from 41 to 44. A sample of
approximately 50 per cent of the cases was taken by recording the appropriate values on the left-hand side of the census manuscript books.

One of the surprising aspects of Table 22 is the large inequality
within each nationality group. The nine Gini coefficients for the nine
foreign-country classifications have a median value of 0.670, not very
much less than the 0.691 for all foreign born. Only for such small na-
tions as Wales, Holland, and the Scandinavian countries, are coefficients near 0.6. One thinks of Norwegian staging centers for the newly
arrived when he sees that each nationality group included persons with
no wealth. Analysis of the Gini R's for the five main domestic groups
of the table indicates essentially the same results as those for foreign
born. The median of 0.685 is near that of 0.699 for all native born.

The various means and medians for Wisconsin nativity groups do
not demonstrate differences so dramatic as those existing in the city
of Milwaukee in 1860. New England nativity groups had a mean of
about \$3,000. Groups from England, Wales, and Scotland had means
of about \$2,000, from Germany and Ireland of \$1,000, and from the
Scandinavian countries of \$800. The mean nativity gradient within the
United States is interesting. It is \$3,200 for the east coast, \$2,800
for Pennsylvania and Ohio, and \$1,600 for the Middle West. The \$900
figure for the 33 born in Wisconsin is inexplicable since they were
scattered among many counties except in Milwaukee, where there were
9. The mean nativity gradient for the United States must have been a
reflection of the nativity of parents and grandparents discussed previously in the Milwaukee analysis. The arithmetic mean is strongly
influenced by affluent groups, particularly a few merchants and lawyers.
The median, however, is representative of the middle of the rung and
its gradient for native-born groups is not nearly so strong. The typical
person born in Indiana, Illinois, and Michigan had almost the same
wealth as a typical (median) person born in Maine, New Hampshire,
and Vermont.

A separate analysis was made by county of some of the main measures for the study of 40-year olds. The number of cases, mean, and
Gini R for all native-born, foreign-born, and German-born subsets for
each of the 58 counties was determined. A multiple regression analysis
has been made of the 33 counties having at least 10 cases in each cell.
This means that the frontier counties have been eliminated, since no
county included has less than 9 persons per square mile. Of the 25
counties eliminated, only 5 had a density greater than 9. Many of the
results obtained from this study of 40-year olds are similar to those
obtained for all-age groups in 1860 with appreciable density, so they
need not be discussed at length.

For averages where NB is native born, FB is foreign born, Ger is
German born, all is $NB + FB$, 40 is for age 40, all age is for all males
20 and up, n is the number of cases of 33, s_b is the standard error of
the regression coefficient, and r^2 is the coefficient of correlation
squared:

$$\log \bar{X}_{all,40} = -0.9200 + 1.3177 \log \bar{X}_{all,all\ ages}, \quad n = 33, \quad r^2 = 0.77,$$
$$s_b = 0.1280$$

$$\log \bar{X}_{NB,40} = -0.9505 + 1.3583 \log \bar{X}_{all,40}, \quad n = 33, \quad r^2 = 0.77,$$
$$s_b = 0.1322$$

$$\log \bar{X}_{FB,40} = 1.0274 + 0.6215 \log \bar{X}_{all,40}, \quad n = 33, \quad r^2 = 0.52,$$
$$s_b = 0.1076$$

$$\log \bar{X}_{Ger,40} = 1.3296 + 0.5010 \log \bar{X}_{all,40}, \quad n = 33, \quad r^2 = 0.20,$$
$$s_b = 0.1775$$

$$\log \bar{X}_{all,all\ ages} = 1.2444 + 0.5872 \log \bar{X}_{all,40}, \quad n = 33, \quad r^2 = 0.77,$$
$$s_b = 0.0570.$$

The arithmetic mean for 40-year olds was relatively elastic with respect to average wealth in a county. A 40-year-old had, on the average,
13.2 per cent more wealth than another individual if he lived in a
county having 10 per cent more wealth. Elasticities with respect to
$\bar{X}_{all,40}$ show that a native born had a higher relative wealth average
if he lived in a rich county than if he lived in a poor one. This is not
true of foreign born; the elasticity was even smaller for German born.

Detailed study of a Norwegian city in the 1860's shows it to have
had greater inequality than in Milwaukee and even much greater inequality than among Norwegians living in Wisconsin. The very rich
in the Norwegian city had substantially more than the Wisconsin Norwegians, but the break-even level was at the 80th or 90th percentile.

Table 22. Distribution of Wealth of Males 40 Years Old, Classified by the Country or Region of Birth, Wisconsin, 1860

Lower-class limit in dollars	Me. N.H. Vt.	Conn. Mass. R.I.	N.Y. N.J. Del.	Penn.	Ohio	Ind. Ill. Mich.
	Number of males			$(L_X$ = cumulative per cent of cases)		
0–	37 (16)	13 (10)	85 (11)	15 (13)	9 (8)	7 (17)
10–	3 (17)	4 (13)	17 (14)	3 (15)	4 (11)	1 (20)
100–	10 (21)	5 (17)	41 (19)	7 (21)	6 (16)	2 (24)
200–	19 (29)	9 (24)	63 (28)	16 (34)	14 (28)	3 (32)
500–	29 (42)	21 (40)	91 (40)	18 (50)	22 (46)	6 (46)
1,000–	50 (63)	23 (57)	159 (61)	22 (68)	25 (67)	11 (73)
2,000–	46 (82)	31 (81)	186 (86)	18 (83)	22 (86)	7 (90)
5,000–	26 (93)	16 (93)	61 (94)	16 (97)	12 (96)	4 (100)
10,000–	9 (97)	6 (98)	24 (98)	2 (98)	1 (97)	0
20,000–	6 (100)	3 (100)	12 (99)	1 (99)	3 (99)	0
50,000–	1 (100)		3 (100)	1 (100)	1 (100)	0
100,000–			1 (100)			
200,000–			1 (100)			
	236	131	744	119	119	41
Mean	$3,156	3,214	3,254	2,804	2,845	1,656
Median	1,265	1,400	1,300	1,000	1,150	1,070
Gini R	0.685	0.647	0.705	0.710	0.682	0.586

Lower-class limit in dollars	Wis.	Ky. Tenn. Md.	Va., N.C. S.C., Ga. Miss.	Other native born	England	Wales
	Number of males			$(L_X$ = cumulative per cent of cases)		
0–	18 (55)	5 (19)	1 (14)	0	53 (16)	16 (19)
10–	0	2 (26)	2 (43)	2 (50)	12 (20)	4 (24)
100–	1 (57)	3 (37)	2 (72)	0	19 (26)	5 (30)
200–	5 (73)	0	1 (86)	0	53 (43)	6 (37)
500–	3 (82)	1 (41)	0	1 (75)	36 (54)	10 (49)
1,000–	2 (88)	10 (78)	1 (100)	1 (100)	66 (74)	18 (70)
2,000–	3 (97)	5 (96)			61 (93)	19 (93)
5,000–	0	1 (100)			12 (97)	4 (98)
10,000–	1 (100)	0			5 (99)	2 (100)
20,000–	0	0			3 (100)	
50,000–	0	0			2 (100)	
100,000–						
200,000–						
	33	27	7	4	322	84
Mean	$902	1,313	329	422	2,112	1,685
Median	0	1,050	100	275	700	1,050
Gini R	0.846	0.579	0.693	0.536	0.729	0.615

(continued)

Table 22 (continued)

Lower-class limit in dollars	Scotland	Switzerland	Canada, Brit. America	Germany	Ireland	Norway Sweden Denmark
	Number of males			(L_X = cumulative per cent of cases)		
0–	17 (19)	6 (15)	23 (25)	200 (20)	175 (20)	44 (19)
10–	2 (21)	2 (20)	6 (31)	69 (27)	59 (26)	12 (25)
100–	2 (23)	3 (28)	6 (38)	62 (33)	67 (34)	20 (34)
200–	9 (33)	4 (38)	15 (54)	151 (48)	137 (49)	37 (50)
500–	15 (49)	7 (56)	21 (76)	216 (70)	166 (68)	40 (67)
1,000–	19 (70)	6 (72)	11 (89)		167 (86)	47 (88)
2,000–	20 (92)	7 (90)	6 (95)	181 (88)	103 (98)	25 (99)
5,000–	6 (98)	1 (92)	4 (99)	97 (97)	14 (99)	1 (100)
10,000–	0	3 (100)	0	21 (99)	5 (100)	1 (100)
20,000–	2 (100)		1 (100)	4 (100)	0	0
50,000–				2 (100)	1 (100)	
100,000–				1 (100)		
200,000–						
	92	39	93	1,004	894	227
Mean	$2,154	2,058	1,202	1,038	1,009	811
Median	$1,000	650	350	500	500	500
Gini R	0.670	0.689	0.757	0.679	0.663	0.607

Lower-class limit in dollars	Holland	Other foreign born	Total native born	Total foreign born	Total of native and foreign born
	Number of males		(L_X = cumulative per cent of cases)		
0–	9 (21)	17 (17)	190 (13)	560 (19)	750 (17)
10–	0	7 (24)	38 (16)	173 (25)	211 (22)
100–	2 (26)	8 (32)	77 (21)	194 (32)	271 (28)
200–	11 (51)	26 (57)	130 (30)	449 (47)	579 (42)
500–	13 (82)	21 (78)	192 (43)	545 (66)	737 (58)
1,000–	5 (93)	10 (88)	304 (64)	530 (84)	834 (78)
2,000–	3 (100)	6 (94)	318 (85)	347 (96)	665 (93)
5,000		6 (100)	136 (95)	69 (99)	205 (98)
10,000–		0	43 (98)	20 (99)	63 (99)
20,000–		0	25 (99)	8 (100)	33 (100)
50,000–			6 (100)	4 (100)	10 (100)
100,000–			1 (100)	0	1 (100)
200,000–			1 (100)	0	1 (100)
	43	101	1,461	2,899	4,360
Mean	$602	932	3,016	1.193	1,802
Median	$450	400	1,200	500	610
Gini R	0.548	0.691	0.699	0.691	0.719

Source: Schedule 1 of the 1860 Census.

Below this value, Wisconsin Norwegians had greater wealth. What more might an ordinary immigrant wish than less inequality and a much higher wealth average? Investigation of three Norwegian-dominated townships in Wisconsin and Minnesota for 1860 indicates a great area diversity of land holdings and distribution. Some groups were more fortunate than others. On the wider scene in Wisconsin, we found those born in England, Wales, and Scotland to have wealth averages twice those born in Germany and Ireland who, in turn, had one fourth larger averages than those born in Scandinavia. Those native born living in Wisconsin who were born on the east coast had higher mean, but not median, average wealth than those born further west.

We return now in Chapters 6 and 7 to our search for changes in wealth and income distribution in Milwaukee and Wisconsin after 1870.

Chapter 6

Wealth Distributions
After 1870

In this chapter, inheritance tax data for 1900, 1927—28, 1936, and 1963 will be examined along with certain aggregate wealth estimates from 1850 to 1922 and mortgage distributions from 1880 to 1890. There will then follow a discussion of four institutions, both subsuming and subsumed by the field of wealth: inheritance transmission, decreased migration coupled with age-nativity changes, education, and land settlement. All will be discussed in terms of long-run changes.

A. WEALTH DISTRIBUTIONS

After 1870 there was no general census of individual wealth in Milwaukee County or in Wisconsin. One must resort to four studies in the years 1900, 1927—28, 1936, and 1963, which give only a partial picture of wealth distributions. The first of these is a distribution of estate values of males for six counties, including Milwaukee County, in 1900. The estate values of the deceased obviously represent an age group much older than that of the labor force as a whole. There is a distribution of estates in Wisconsin for the year 1927—28 with remarkable detail about how the estate totals were distributed among heirs; one can gain some insights into how the inheritance mechanism worked at this time. Data for 1936 and 1963 similar to the 1927—28 data will be examined briefly. The examination of wealth changes is concluded by presenting mortgage debt distributions for the decade from 1880 to 1890. Let us begin by looking at census estimates of aggregate wealth, including real estate, for Wisconsin every tenth year from 1850 to 1900 and for the years 1904, 1912, and 1922.

1. *Aggregate Wealth Estimates in Wisconsin, 1860 to 1922*

For many years the Bureau of the Census of the Department of Commerce made estimates of all tangible property in the various states. This involved an attempt to arrive at the "true" value of real and personal property, a measure introduced in Chapter 2, using the abbreviation VEOT. The evolution of published detail for the measure is shown in Table 23 using Wisconsin data for 1860, 1890, and 1912. One can trace in this table the decreased relative importance of real estate over a half century and the increased importance of manufacturing and utilities.

Decennial wealth aggregates from 1850 to 1900 plus aggregates for 1904, 1912, and 1922 have been made. No later estimates by state were published. In producing per capita wealth values over time, one is faced with a difficult deflating problem; Exhibit 18 gives values deflated by the Bureau of Labor Statistics consumer price indexes, which are presented in Appendix 3.

The least-squares trend equation for the 8 points from 1860 to 1922 is $W = \$429 \ (1.024)^t$, $t = 0$ in 1860, where W is per capita wealth in 1860 dollars. One wonders if 2.4 per cent might not overstate the magnitude of growth in real capital per capita. One possible correction would be to apply the ratio of total population to the population of males 20 years old and over which in Wisconsin was: 1860, 3.89; 1880, 3.71; 1890, 3.55; 1900, 3.51; 1910, 3.30; and 1920, 3.20. The exponential trend of these data is minus 0.32 per cent per annum. This correction applied to the 2.4 per cent coefficient of the chart would yield almost the 2 per cent value found earlier in the study.

However, one should not press the 2 per cent growth figure unduly. For example, the 1850 value for the Wisconsin data has not been included in the calculation of trend. It is instructive to examine United States data in this connection. Wealth in current dollars per capita was:

	1850	1860	1870	1880	1890
United States	308	514	780	870	1,036
Wisconsin	138	353	666	866	1,087

This is essentially valuation according to location rather than ownership.[1] The United States value of $308 for 1850 would have been in line with the Wisconsin trend extrapolation for that year.

2. *Estates in 1900 in Six Counties in Wisconsin*

Max Lorenz made a study of the value of male estates in six Wisconsin counties in 1900 which has been reported by Dr. Willford King, after making certain adjustments for underreporting.[2] The population of the counties was:

Table 23. Estimates of National Wealth, Wisconsin, 1860, 1890, 1912

Year	Wisconsin (in thousands of dollars)	Wisconsin (per cent of total)
1860:		
Assessed value		
Total	$185,845[a]	100.0
Real estate	148,238	79.7
Personal estate	37,706	20.3
Total true value of real and		
personal estate	273,671	
1890:		
True valuation of real estate and		
improvements		
Total	1,098,350[a]	—
Taxed	1,022,794	—
Exempt from taxation	75,555	—
True valuation of real and		
personal property		
Total	1,833,308[a]	100
Real estate and improvements	1,098,350	59.9
Livestock on farms, farm imple-		
ments and machinery	82,951	4.5
Mines and quarries, including		
product on hand	8,388	0.5
Gold and silver coin and bullion	27,934	1.5
Machinery of mills and product on		
hand, raw and manufactured	81,874	4.5
Railroads and equipment, in-		
cluding street cars	294,269	16.1
Telegraphs, telephones, and		
shipping and canals and equipment	14,738	0.8
Miscellaneous	224,801	12.3
1912:		
True value of all property		
Total	4,487,725[a]	100
Real property and improvements	2,503,171	55.8
Livestock	229,489	5.1
Farm implements and machinery	57,700	1.3
Manufacturing machinery, tools,		
implements	163,224	3.6
Gold and silver coin and bullion	50,200	1.1
Railroads and their equipment	480,673	10.7
Street railways, shipping, water		
works, etc.	146,742	3.3
All other	856,522	19.1

[a]Figures in these columns do not add to totals because of rounding.

Source: U.S. Census Office. 8th Census, 1860. *Statistics of the United States (Including Mortality, Property, &c.,) in 1860* (GPO: Washington, D.C., 1866), pp. 294, 295; U.S. Census Office. 11th Census. Vol. 15, *Wealth, Debt, and Taxation*, 2 vols. (GPO: Washington, D.C., 1892–95), pp. 12–15; U.S. Department of Commerce, Bureau of Foreign and Domestic Commerce, *Statistical Abstract of the United States*, No. 42, 1919 (GPO: Washington, D.C., 1919), p. 702.

Exhibit 18
Per Capita Wealth and Income in Wisconsin for Selected Years, 1860–1960[a]

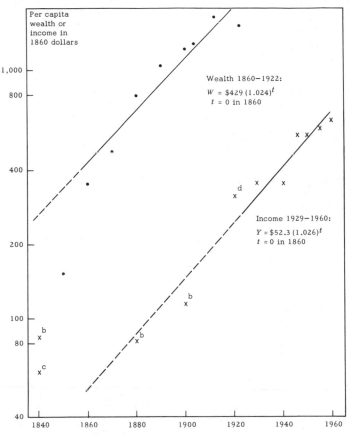

[a]All data deflated with price indices of Appendix 3.
[b]Estimate of Richard Easterlin, "Trends in the American Economy in the Nineteenth Century," in National Bureau of Economic Research, *Studies in Income and Wealth*, Vol. 24 (Princeton, N.J., 1960), pp. 98, 99, 102.
[c]Estimate of George Tucker, *Progress of the United States in Population and Wealth in Fifty Years* (New York, 1843), pp. 192–95.
[d]Estimate of Maurice Leven, *Income in the Various States* (National Bureau of Economic Research, 1925), p. 256.

Sources: 1850–1890 wealth figures, U.S. Census Office. 11th Census, 1890. Vol. 15, *Wealth, Debt, and Taxation*, 2 vols. (Washington, D.C., 1892–95), p. 14; 1890–1922 wealth figures, U.S. Dept. of Commerce, *Statistical Abstract of the United States 1936* (Washington, D.C., 1936), p. 273; 1840 income, Tucker, *Progress of the United States in Population and Wealth in Fifty Years*, pp. 192–95, with a per capita division correction; 1840, 1880, and 1900 income, Easterlin, "Trends in the American Economy in the Nineteenth Century," pp. 98, 99, 102; 1919–1920 income, Leven, *Income in the Various States*, p. 256; 1929, 1940, 1950, 1955, and 1960 income, *Survey of Current Business*, April, 1965, p. 19.

	Male population 21 years old and over in 1900
Dane	19,972
Grant	10,652
Manitowoc	11,028
Milwaukee	88,986
Racine	13,165
Winnebago	16,107
Six-county total	159,892
Wisconsin	570,715

Milwaukee's population was 56 per cent times that of the 6 counties which, in turn, was 28 per cent times that of the state's population.

For deaths, Wisconsin data[3] show that, even in a rapidly growing population, the great majority of deaths occur in older groups:

Age	Wisconsin male deaths reported in 1900	Wisconsin male population in 1900	Deaths per thousand males in 1900
20—24	503	91,204	5.5
25—29	481	82,594	5.8
30—34	455	76,358	6.0
35—39	489	72,464	6.7
40—44	534	64,084	8.3
45—49	476	49,158	9.7
50—54	534	40,381	13.2
55—59	604	31,692	19.1
60—64	624	25,228	24.7
65 & up	4,058	54,644	74.2
	8,758	587,807	
20 & up	8,758	587,807	14.9
25 & up	8,255	496,603	16.6
50 & up	5,820	151,945	38.3

Thus, among males 20 years old and over in 1900, two thirds of the deaths were among those who were 50 years old and over. We would expect then that a distribution of estate values not explicitly standardized for age groups would largely reflect economic conditions of those having been in the labor force more than half of their working years. The classifications in the top half of Table 24 should be viewed in that light.

The data of Dr. King show a total number of estates of 2,332 for males 25 and over in the 6 counties. Presumably this was obtained by applying the per cent of Wisconsin population in the 6 counties (of 28) to Wisconsin total deaths above age 25, or 8,255. Estates not reported apparently had been placed in the class from $0 to $500 and

Table 24. Distribution of Estate Values of Deceased Males 25 Years Old and Over, Six Wisconsin Counties Including Milwaukee County, 1900, and Distribution of Wealth of Males 50 Years Old and Over, Milwaukee County, 1860.

Value of estate (lower class limit or X)	Number of estates in 1900	Amount of estates (in thousands of dollars)	Arithmetic mean of all estates above X	Concentration coefficient of all estates above X, R_X
$ 0–	1,570	589	$ 4,800	0.84
500–	74	53	13,800	.72
1,000–	165	286	15,200	.70
2,500–	161	633	19,500	.66
5,000–	108	607	26,400	.64
7,500–	75	617	35,200	.62
10,000–	66	788	46,500	.60
15,000–	50	845	66,700	.57
25,000–	33	1,116	106,000	
50,000–	12	835	186,000	
100,000–	16	3,492	263,000	
500,000–	2	1,244	622,000	
	2,322	11,105		

Wealth value (lower- class limit or X)	Number of wealth- holders in 1860	Amount of wealth (in thousands of dollars)[a]	Arithmetic mean of all holders above X	Concentration coefficient of all holders above X, R_X
$ 0–	1,340	90	$ 3,700	0.88
500–	320	196	7,500	.77
1,000–	460	723	9,900	.74
2,500–	220	750	18,200	.69
5,000–	80	505	31,400	.64
7,500–	40	360	43,600	.60
10,000–	40	456	54,500	.56
15,000–	20	424	74,600	.49
25,000–	26	791	90,800	
50,000–	25	1,659	130,000	
100,000–	13	2,395	236,000	
500,000–	2	1,145	572,500	
	2,586	9,494		

[a]Consumer prices in 1900 were 95 per cent of those in 1860.

Sources: 1860 wealth data, Schedule 1 of the 1860 Census for Milwaukee County; 1900 data, Willford King, *Wealth and Income of the People of the United States* (New York, 1915), p. 76, as adapted from a manuscript study by Max Lorenz, "The Distribution of Wealth in Six Wisconsin Counties" (Dane, Grant, Manitowoc, Milwaukee, Racine, and Winnebago). These data are also available in Richard T. Ely, *Property and Contract in their Relation to the Distribution of Wealth* (New York, 1914), Vol. I, pp. 312–13.

given an average value near $500. Table 24 shows the concentration
coefficient where data from 5 or more classes exist. The overall coefficient is reminiscent of the 0.89 wealth value for Milwaukee County
in 1860.

Some measure of the change in wealth concentration from 1860 to
1900 could be obtained from the Milwaukee data if a group comparable
to that in 1900 could be chosen from the 1860 set. Unfortunately, the
King data of 1900 are classified neither by nativity nor by age. It was
decided to choose the group 50 years old and over in 1860 for comparison purposes rather than to develop some composite of various 1860
age groups. This is done in the lower half of Table 24. One easily
notes the very strong similarity between the 1860 and 1900 distributions. The ratio (frequency$_{1860}$/frequency$_{1900}$) for the 12 classes is
1.0, 0.8, 2.1, 0.8, 0.4, 0.6, 0.5, 0.7, 1.4, 2.8, 4.3, and 0.9, in descend-
ing from the highest to lowest wealth classes. The last three ratios
dealing with low wealth classes may be combined in one class yielding a ratio of 1.2. The factor of 1 is coincidence since the one case
is for the living, in 1 county, and the other is for deaths 40 years
later, in 6 counties. However, the consistency of the frequency ratios
is very significant. The concentration coefficients and averages are
not essentially different in the two years. Any discrepancies could
almost be explained by the midpoint assumption in the $0 to $500
class.

One concludes that among older persons, no undue "birth of barons"
took place in the push to industrialization. There is no group of multi-
millionaires in the 1900 data. It is very true that economic growth
expanded to the point where the number of deaths of the wealthy in
1900 equalled the total number of wealthy 40 years earlier. The implication is that the deaths in 1900 were a subset of many rich people
since the number of males 50 and up in Milwaukee County was almost
7 times as large in 1900 as in 1860. Thus, the top 100 persons in 1900
would have far greater wealth than the top 100 persons in 1860.

The average wealth above the lower class limits of the 1900 and
1860 groups in Table 24 appears to be about the same for 10 of the 12
classes. One may draw two inverse Pareto curves, parallel to each
other but with one showing 7 times as many people above a given dollar limit. If this is done with our data, one concludes that the top 100
persons had approximately 8 times as much wealth in 1900 as in 1860.
The factor of 8 would also apply to any other absolute number of people. Values need not be corrected for price changes since consumer
prices in 1900 were 95 per cent those in 1860.

One is not in a position to assert that inequality of wealth remained
constant in the last half of the nineteenth century in Milwaukee or in
Wisconsin. The data observed are only for older persons. It may be
very likely that the young received an increasing share. Some further
observations on this point will be made later in the chapter.

3. *Estates in Wisconsin in 1927–28*

Data for 3,315 inheritance tax orders made in 1927–28 are shown in
Table 25. Several qualifications of the distribution should be noted.
The first is that the estates are those of both males and females. The
second is that the exemption levels were $15,000 for the wife of a de-
cedent, $2,000 for the husband, and lesser amounts for the other de-
scendents. The statistics reflect these limits. For example, the distribution of transfers to widows shows a discontinuity at $15,000. The
number of Wisconsin males 20 and over dying in 1927 was 12,803, or
9,488 more than the 3,315 reports. There were 407 estates listing
transfer to wives among the 3,315 reports. An entry of 10,000 is made
in Table 25 to cover these cases in deriving essentially a male distribution of decedents.

The concentration coefficient for estates in 1927–28 of 0.806 is not
dissimilar from that obtained for Wisconsin males in 1860. An analysis
made of estates for 1936 leads to the same conclusion.[4] Considering
the qualifications of the data, there does not seem to be evidence of
more inequality in 1927–28 in Wisconsin than in 1860 for this older
group. Indeed, there may have been 10 per cent less inequality. The
exemption level of $15,000 in 1927 was roughly the price equivalent
of $7,500 in 1860 and 1900. One notes an R of 0.50 above $15,000 for
Wisconsin in 1927–28 and R's of 0.60 and 0.62 above $7,500 in 1860
and 1900, respectively, for the counties of Table 24. Another interesting aspect is that the arithmetic mean of the estates is no larger, and
in real dollars may have been smaller, than the values in 1900 and
1860. Perhaps the young were sharing more extensively in economic
growth.

4. *Estates Over $60,000 in Wisconsin in 1963*

One now turns to Federal data for estates filed in the year 1963.
Unfortunately, the exemption level of $60,000 means that the informa-
tion presented in Exhibit 19 is only for those who were rich. The total
number of estates is only between 5 and 10 per cent of 33,590, the
number of males and females 45 years old or over dying in Wisconsin
in 1962.

Least-squares equations for the points of Exhibit 19 and two other
situations are:

1963 $60,000 \leq X \leq \$5,000,000$ $N = 16$, Wisconsin

$$X = \$7,700,000 \, L_X^{-0.659}$$ (L_X is for taxable
                                                                returns)

1927–28 $10,000 \leq X \leq \$1,000,000$ $N = 15$, Wisconsin

$$X = \$1,890,000 \, L_X^{-0.683}$$

Table 25. Distribution of Estate Values Subject to Inheritance Taxation for
Wisconsin, June 30, 1927, to June 30, 1928

Net value of estate (lower-class limit or X)	Number of estates in 1927–28	Net value of estates (in thousands of dollars)	Arithmetic mean of all estates above X	Concentration coefficient of all holders above X, R_X
$ 0–	10,000[a]	6,580[b]	$ 5,600	0.806
0–	57	37	20,600	.628
1,000–	119	176	20,900	.623
2,000–	291	733	21,700	.613
3,000–	226	788	23,600	.591
4,000–	234	1,051	25,400	.575
5,000–	216	1,188	27,400	.560
6,000–	160	1,044	29,600	.546
7,000–	160	1,195	31,400	.537
8,000–	142	1,210	33,500	.527
9,000–	136	1,289	35,600	.519
10,000–	800	11,510	37,800	.511
20,000–	343	8,362	62,100	.494
30,000–	154	5,288	92,100	.489
40,000–	72	3,205	124,000	.476
50,000–	36	1,974	152,000	.460
60,000–	40	2,556	173,000	.450
70,000–	17	1,280	207,000	.433
80,000–	17	1,438	227,000	.422
90,000–	11	1,049	252,000	.409
100,000–	49	6,861	272,000	.399
200,000–	19	4,501	458,000	.393
300,000–	6	2,064	722,000	.398
400,000–	4	1,800	948,000	.392
500,000–	2	1,087	1,280,000	.376
600,000–	0			
700,000–	1	757	1,650,000	—
800,000–	1	855	1,940,000	—
900,000–	0			
1,000,000–	1	1,660	2,490,000	—
2,000,000–	0	—	—	—
3,000,000–	1	3,318	3,320,000	—
	13,315	74,870[c]		

[a]The 10,000 is an estimate for the number of deceased males, age 20 and above,
not accounted for by the 3,315 taxable estates.
[b]The average income given is the same as that reported for the 57 cases below
$1,000.
[c]Figures in this column do not add to total because of rounding.

Source: *Report of the Wisconsin Tax Commission to the Governor and Legislature* (Madison, Wis., 1928), p. 196.

Exhibit 19

Inverse Pareto Curves[a] for Wisconsin Estates in 1927 and 1963, for Estates of
Males in Six Wisconsin Counties in 1900, and for Wealth of Males 50 Years Old
and Over in Wisconsin and Milwaukee in 1860

X, or wealth in
current dollars

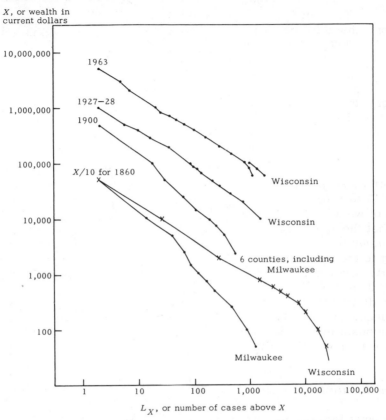

L_X, or number of cases above X

[a]Points shown are for taxable returns. Data for taxable plus non-taxable returns at $100,000, $80,000, and $60,000 are shown as three separate points.

Source: U.S. Department of Commerce, *Statistics of Income, Fiduciary, Gift, and
Estate Tax Returns, 1962* (Washington, D.C., 1965), p. 78.

1900 $2,500 \le X \le $500,000 N = 9, 6 counties, in-
                                                                      cluding Milwaukee
                        $X = $1,160,000 \, L_X^{-0.930}$

1860 for   those 50 and over
                 $800 \le X \le $500,000 N = 12, Wisconsin

                        $X = $914,000 \, L_X^{-0.666}$

1860 for   those 50 and over
        $800 \leq X \leq$ \$500,000 $N = 11$, Milwaukee
                                                 County

$$X = \$1,700,000 \, L_X^{-1.073}$$

1850 for   those 50 and over
        $800 \leq X \leq$ \$200,000 $N = 12$, Wisconsin

$$X = \$270,000 \, L_X^{-0.670}$$

1860 for   those 20 and over
        $1,000 \leq X \leq$ \$500,000 $N = 9$, Wisconsin

$$X = \$1,390,000 \, L_X^{-0.618}$$

It can be seen that there is at most a 5 per cent drop in the slope from 1927 to 1963. There is very little evidence of change in concentration of wealth demonstrated from these data, but again one must state that these figures are limited to the range above \$60,000 in 1963 and \$10,000 in 1927. There is internal consistency between the lines leading to the implication of a 1.6 per cent growth rate per annum in the thirty-six-year period for this limited group of persons.[5] As stated earlier, there is little or no evidence of change between the 1860 Milwaukee distribution and the 1900 six-county distribution dominated by Milwaukee. Finally, there is little or no difference between the slopes for Wisconsin in 1927 and 1963 pertaining to estates of deceased and the slopes for Wisconsin in 1860 and 1850 for those 50 years old and over.[6]

5. *Real Estate Mortgages in Milwaukee and Wisconsin, 1880–1890*

One must look diligently to find data having bearing on wealth distribution between 1870 and 1900. This is sometimes thought to be the very crucial period when increased inequality might have taken place, so even debt configurations prove to be of value. A source of information which seems of significance is an elaborate study of mortgages made by the Bureau of the Census covering the period from 1880 to 1890 for the United States.[7]

Distributions of the value of debt are available for Wisconsin and Milwaukee County. Summaries are presented in Table 26. In general, these data do not include mortgages made by quasi-public corporations such as railroads, telegraphs, and public water companies. Since the life of a mortgage was about four years, the mortgage debt outstanding represents only about 12 per cent of real estate in the case of Wisconsin and 23 per cent in the case of Milwaukee. Yet it was a dynamic part. Over 80 per cent of the mortgages were obtained for the purpose

Table 26. Distribution of Real Estate Mortgage Values Made in Milwaukee and Wisconsin, 1880–1889

Distributions of Values Made in the Years 1880 and 1889

Milwaukee County

Lower-class limit	1880 Number	1880 Amount	1889 Number	1889 Amount
$ 0–	22	$ 1,271	53	$ 3,104
100–	171	20,728	358	42,470
200–	314	68,698	445	96,941
300–	244	77,684	514	163,653
400–	217	89,515	456	189,297
500–	489	313,864	1,644	1,081,626
1,000–	201	222,433	843	938,823
1,500–	93	148,135	347	556,634
2,000–	92	190,838	232	481,340
2,500–	105	344,009	388	1,259,585
5,000–	61	373,184	140	862,042
10,000–	18	206,057	55	603,775
15,000–	4	63,000	17	277,271
20,000–	4	83,500	14	289,500
25,000–			18	618,875
50,000–	1	50,000	5	294,000
100,000–	0	—	0	—
500,000–	0	—	0	—
	2,036	2,252,916	5,529	7,758,936
$\overline{X}$		$1,106		$1,403
Gini R		0.605		0.600

Wisconsin

Lower-class limit	1880 Number	1880 Amount	1889 Number	1889 Amount
$ 0–	1,463	$ 87,909	1,739	$ 104,894
100–	4,163	557,774	5,549	710,174
200–	3,718	328,570	4,782	1,060,857
300–	2,789	885,789	3,791	1,207,785
400–	1,907	792,379	2,840	1,178,192
500–	5,424	3,487,020	8,220	5,309,405
1,000–	2,426	2,692,020	3,703	4,125,226
1,500–	880	1,422,181	1,538	2,470,170
2,000–	633	1,315,365	1,198	2,484,724
2,500–	768	2,442,546	1,706	5,482,119
5,000–	191	1,186,712	479	2,905,372
10,000–	37	412,549	111	1,234,975
15,000–	11	175,380	35	563,634
20,000–	6	125,500	25	534,081
25,000–	4	127,767	32	1,037,208
50,000–	9	481,455	8	461,000
100,000–	1	148,433	2	500,000
500,000–	0	—	0	—
	24,430	17,169,349[a]	35,758	31,372,816[a]
$\overline{X}$		$703		$877
Gini R		0.560		0.595

(continued)

Table 26 (continued)

	Mean and Concentration Coefficients, 1880–1889					
	Milwaukee County		Wisconsin		United States	
	Mean	Gini R	Mean	Gini R	Mean	Gini R
1880	$1,106	0.605	$702	0.560	$1,105	0.642
1881	1,164	.619	759	.582	1,184	.650
1882	1,186	.630	834	.600	1,262	.656
1883	1,158	.611	848	.610	1,243	.650
1884	1,140	.598	794	.600	1,227	.652
1885	1,172	.594	734	.581	1,164	.638
1886	1,196	.588	795	.599	1,241	.652
1887	1,349	.606	903	.624	1,347	.658
1888	1,488	.624	875	.600	1,353	.663
1889	1,403	.600	877	.595	1,429	.666

[a]Figures in these columns do not add to totals because of rounding.

Source: U.S. Census Bureau. 11th Census, 1890. *Mortgages*, Vol. XII (GPO: Washington, 1897), Tables 7, 19, 108.

of acquiring land. Little evidence of hardship was found even though the survey grew out of widespread discontent of farmers and working-men. One is dealing with a segment of real estate which was changing hands rapidly and could play a major part in the change in wealth inequality. It was an indicator of changes in inequality in personal estate to the extent that mortgage debt was incurred to buy stock or to invest in business. It was also a measure of mortgages held as part of personal estate.

If one examines the Gini coefficients of Table 26 and notes their remarkable constancy, he must conclude that there was no change in inequality in the decade prior to 1890. Surprisingly, relative inequality of mortgage debt in the urban areas was no larger in Milwaukee County than it was in the state. Lot ownership in cities was the counterpart to farm ownership in rural areas, at least in part. The number of mortgages on lots per capita increased 6 per cent per annum from 1880 to 1889 in Milwaukee and 5 per cent outside of Milwaukee. The number of mortgages on acres remained constant in this period in the state.

B. FACTORS AFFECTING WEALTH

We now introduce the mechanism of inheritance and estate transmission, after which we will discuss four changes in institutions of wealth, namely, changes in population, age, nativity, education, and land distribution. The income supplement in the final chapter contains observations about income distribution which are related to wealth distribution.

1. *Inheritances in Wisconsin, 1927–28*

The value of the 1927–28 data already presented is that they allow an analysis of the way in which estates were transferred to the various heirs. A plot of the estate points was shown earlier to unfold as an excellent inverse-Pareto curve above $10,000. A plot of the transfers unfolds as the same general shape with linearity to $2,000. The equations are:

1927–28 estates $\$10,000 \leq X \leq \$1,000,000$; $N = 15$, Wisconsin

$$\log X = 6.2769 - 0.6826 \log L_X$$

1927–28 transfers $\$2,000 \leq X \leq \$1,000,000$; $N = 9$, Wisconsin

$$\log X = 6.1424 - 0.6993 \log L_X.$$

The two equations are parallel to each other, with that for transfers being at a wealth level about 70 per cent of that for estates, for a given value of L_X. Alternatively, the number of estates is about two thirds larger than the number of transfers for a given value of X. If we limit ourselves only to the transfers to children of the decedents, we find again the same Pareto slope but a curve anchored at an even lower level.

These are quantifications of the dissolutions of estates because of a greater number of beneficiaries than decedents. The values for slopes mean that relative inequality was left intact by the transfers. It would, however, take at least a few years on the average for the beneficiaries to build the inheritances back to the levels of the original estates. And this process would lead only to the perpetuation of an elite of the same absolute size, not one of an expanding population. A family with three children necessarily suffers some retardation in wealth accumulation from one generation to the next.

2. *Age, Nativity, and Education*

It was shown in Chapters 2 and 3 that there was a very strong relationship between age-nativity classifications and wealth. It was determined from the expression $W = d(1 + r)^{age}$ that the implicit accumulation rate, r, was 8 per cent a year for men in 1860, being higher for native born than for foreign born. There is evidence that in the United States today it is less.[8] One can explain this and some of the decreased inequality by examining what has happened to age distribution and nativity distribution.

If one looks at nativity for given age groups at a point in time such as 1950, he obtains a fairly accurate picture of the change in nativity if life expectancies of native- and foreign-born persons do not differ to a marked degree. Table 27 fits the scheme since it was seen in 1870 that the 20-year-old group had equal numbers of native and foreign born. If the data of the table are fitted to a straight line equation $Y_a = 1.195 - 0.0079\,a$, $22 \le a \le 97$, where $100\,Y_a$ is the per cent native born at age a in 1950 and $N = 16$. Letting $a = 120$ represents those born in 1830 who were age 30 in 1860 and gives a trend value of $Y_a = 24$ per cent. The 1860 data had specifically 14 per cent native born at age 30. We know from the 1860 data that the decrease means that the very poor are eliminated. If all foreign born are eliminated, one is presumably left with decreased inequality unless there is very substantial inequality in the native-born sector.

Table 27. Nativity of Males, Selected Age Groups, Milwaukee County, 1950

Age	Year in which age was 20	Per cent of white males who were native born
12	—	99.3
17	—	99.3
22	1948	98.8
27	—	97.2
32	1938	97.9
37	—	94.0
42	1928	90.2
47	—	82.8
52	1918	80.7
57	—	71.3
62	1908	68.8
67	—	57.9
72	1898	61.1
77	—	56.1
82	1888	58.0
87	—	42.5
92	1878	50.0
97	1873	50.0

Source: U.S. Bureau of the Census. 17th Census, 1950. *Census of Population: 1950* (GPO: Washington, D.C., 1952), pp. 49–132.

Aside from nativity is the question of age. Exhibit 20 illustrates the dramatic shift in relative supply from the young to the old, particularly after 1910. The distribution of experience is literally less unequal in society today than it was a century ago. If one considers the number of males 20 and over and defines their experience as the number of years lived after age 20, he finds the arithmetic mean to be 26.0 years and R to be 0.356 for Wisconsin males in 1960. In 1860, results for these two measures were 16.7 years and 0.409; in 1910 they were 21.1 years and 0.408.

Finally, we must add the greatest leveller of all, education. One can see from Table 28 that inequality in the amount of education is cut in half in the 60-year time span shown by the data. If the data are fitted to a logarithmic linear equation, the values $\log R = 0.6766 - 1.4379 \log \bar{X}$ are obtained. The average annual change in $\bar{X}$ is 1 per cent as estimated from the equation $\bar{X}_a = (15.7)(1.010)^a$, which was obtained from the $\bar{X}$ data of the table, where a is the age in 1950. The extension of this latter equation for a man of age 32 in 1860 would be a man of age 122 in 1950. This gives an $\bar{X}$ of 4.38 and an R of 0.567. This is four times the R of 0.139 for a 30-year old in 1950. There has been a great equalization of educational experience in the United

Exhibit 20
Number of Males by Age Class in Wisconsin in 1860, 1910, and 1960

Number of males, in thousands,
per 10-year interval

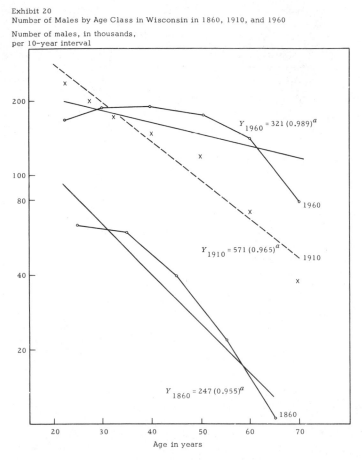

$$Y_{1960} = 321\,(0.989)^a$$

$$Y_{1910} = 571\,(0.965)^a$$

$$Y_{1860} = 247\,(0.955)^a$$

Age in years

Sources: U.S. Census Office. 8th Census, 1860. *Population of the United States
in 1860* (GPO: Washington, D.C., 1864), pp. 526–31; U.S. Bureau of the Census.
16th Census, 1940. Vol. II, *Characteristics of the Population* (GPO: Washington,
D.C., 1943), pp. 49–138; U.S. Bureau of the Census. 18th Census, 1960. Vol. I,
Characteristics of the Population (GPO: Washington, D.C., 1963), pp. 51–299,
51–300.

[a]Age.

States; this may be the proper proxy for measuring the diffusion of
various nationality groups from the last century to this century.
Changes in age, nativity, and education during the last 100 years are
factors tending to reduce inequality of wealth. They may very well
have been sufficient to counteract inequality stemming from the rural
to urban movement.

Table 28. Concentration Coefficients of the
          Amount of Formal Education[a] of
          Males, Classified by Age,
          Milwaukee Standard Metropolitan
          Area, 1950

Age	R	$\bar{X}$
25—29	0.134	11.8
30—34	.139	11.4
35—39	.157	10.6
40—44	.175	10.2
45—54	.198	9.39
55—64	.243	8.06
65—74	.263	7.38
75	.279	7.05

[a]Those with 4 or more years of college
education were assumed to have an average
of 17 years of education.

Source: U.S. Bureau of the Census, 17th
Census, 1950. *Census of Population: 1950*
(GPO: Washington, 1952), pp. 49—154.

3. *The Distribution of Land*

If one were asked to guess how much economic inequality existed
on the frontier in the United States, he probably would answer that
there was little inequality on the basis that in America land was almost free, was abundant relative to population, and was distributed
relatively equally. In fact, however, it is necessary to examine the
inequality of land holdings and to reconcile this distribution with the
very unequal distribution of wealth.

Table 29 shows that in many ways land acreage in Milwaukee
County and in Wisconsin was very "equally" distributed. The concentration coefficients of about 0.40 were similar to those of income distributions today. It is interesting to note that the increase in the number of farms in the two decades after 1850, when accompanied by
further land improvement on existing farms, left the average size and
dispersion of farm lands the same.

Because of its urban economy, discussion of the period after 1870
is better handled by treating Milwaukee County separately from Wisconsin. For Milwaukee, the number of farms as a per cent of adult
males continued to drop until 1959 when their number was insignificant.
The high concentration coefficients in 1959 mean little because of the
relatively large number of farms of a few acres.

In the case of Wisconsin, there is the interesting phenomenon that

Table 29. Distribution of Land in Farms, Milwaukee County and Wisconsin,
Selected Years, 1850—1959

Number of acres	Number of Milwaukee farms					
	1850, improved land	1860,[a] improved land	1870 improved land	1910, farm land	1959, crop land only	1959, all farm land
0–	10		9	54	} 71	146
3–	120	123	205	318		
10–	320	365	360	334	}182	189
20–	490	819	821	813		
50–	210	401	538	678	126	126
100–	40	77	171	246	91	92
500–	0	1	1	0	3	3
1,000–	0	0	0	0	1	1
	1,190	1,786	2,105	2,443	474	557
$\overline{X}$	34 acres	37	43	43	49	59
R	0.40	0.38	0.42	0.43	0.56	0.59
Farms per male population 20 and up	0.135	0.112	0.094[b]	0.018	0.001	0.002

Number of acres	Number of Wisconsin farms				
	1860, improved land	1870, improved land	1910, farm land	1959, crop land only	1959, all farm land
0–		370	273	}1,272	2,713
3–	1,983	5,535	5,491		
10–	9,045	10,955	4,883	}9,806	11,363
20–	30,722	40,064	23,460		
50–	17,826	30,060	54,007	25,108	26,151
100–	9,119	15,776	87,906	87,241	88,695
500–	76	112	966	1,973	2,014
1,000–	11	32	141	272	279
	68,782	102,904	177,127	125,672	131,215
$\overline{X}$	54 acres	57	100	76	153
R	0.40	0.41	0.38	0.29	0.36
Farms per male population 20 and up	0.344	0.387[b]	0.250	0.107	0.112

[a]In 1860, very small farms have been excluded from the published data. In the
Milwaukee County case, the addition of 18 farms of 1 and 2 acres from the 9th Ward
would not have altered the R value of 0.38.

[b]The number of males of 20 years and older in 1870 was estimated as 1.04
times the number 21 and older.

Source: 1850 data, Schedule 4 of the 1850 Census; 1860 data, U.S. Census Office.
8th Census, 1860. *Agriculture of the United States in 1860* (GPO: Washington, D.C.,
1864), pp. 166, 219; 1870 data, U.S. Census Office. 9th Census, 1870. *Agriculture*
(GPO: Washington, D.C., 1872), pp. 280, 366; 1910 data, U.S. Bureau of the Census.
13th Census, 1910. *Abstract: Statistics of Population, Agriculture, Manufactures,
and Mining . . . with Supplement for Wisconsin* (GPO: Washington, D.C., 1913), pp.
641—43; 1959 data, U.S. Bureau of the Census. *Census of Agriculture, 1959* (GPO:
Washington, D.C., 1960), Vol. 1, Parts 14—19, pp. 114—17.

the amount of land per farm increased until 1910 and continued to do
so from 1910 to 1959; the number of farms decreased from 1910 to
1959 and the number per adult male decreased dramatically over the
100-year period. The number of farms per adult male in Wisconsin in
1959 was the same as that in Milwaukee County in 1860. Of special
significance is the decrease in inequality of land holdings. Crop land
shows remarkably low inequality in 1959. One would expect, then,
that farm incomes also might have decreased in inequality.

There are several major difficulties with the statistics and analysis
just given. Some of these were discussed at length in Chapters 3 and
5 for Wisconsin and we shall limit ourselves at this point largely to a
discussion of Milwaukee County. Allowance has been made neither
for farm laborers working for farmers nor for multiple ownership. More
importantly, the value of farm land, determined by its agricultural productivity and alternative non-farm uses, is not reflected in the data.

It is possible to construct a distribution of farm values from the
census reports. One sees in Table 30 that Milwaukee County farms
have a Gini coefficient of 0.44, which is 15 per cent larger than the
coefficient for farm acreage. One considers next the problem of farm
laborers. Of males 20 years old and over sampled in the county,
2,680 were reported as farmers or farm laborers. Also included were
younger men with no occupation listed who were living on farms and
had fathers whose occupation was listed as farmer. The difference

Table 30. Farms Classified by Cash Value, and Farmers and Non-farmers
Classified by Wealth, Milwaukee County, 1860

Cash value of farm (lower class limit)	Number of farms	Lower limit of wealth class	Number of males 20 and up		
			Farmers	Non-farmers	Total
$ 0–	320	0–	1,000	5,480	6,480
1,000–	340	100–	140	1,380	1,520
2,000–	300	200–	240	1,420	1,660
3,000–	200	500–	200	1,660	1,860
4,000–	240	1,000–	380	1,060	1,440
5,000–	120	2,000–	420	640	1,060
6,000–	40	5,000–	240	440	680
7,000–	40	10,000–	40	260	300
8,000–	60	20,000–	14	187	201
10,000–	40	50,000–	5	90	95
14,000–	40	100,000–	1	45	46
	1,740		2,680	12,662	15,342
$\overline{X}$	$3,100	$\overline{X}$	$1,940	2,470	2,380
R	0.44	R	0.725	0.899	0.893
Median	$2,000	Median	$ 430	100	100

Source: Schedules 4 and 1 of the 1860 Census.

between this value and the 1,740 farms is 940. This is taken as the estimate of the non-land-owning labor force.[9] There is some question of whether or not some of these individuals were awaiting transportation or some monies before moving west to farms. In any case, they either stipulated their occupations as farmers or were obviously working on the farms of their fathers. The Gini coefficient for a combination of two groups in which one group owns no land may be obtained[10] by using $R_{1+2} = (n_1 R_1 + n_2)/(n_1 + n_2)$. For Milwaukee land values in 1860, $R_{1+2} = (1,740 \times 0.44 + 940)/(2,680) = 0.64$. A similar calculation for Milwaukee land acreage increases R from 0.38 to 0.62. Importantly, the Wisconsin land acreage R in 1860 increases from 0.40 to 0.67.

Thus one major element in the unequal distribution of land was the farm laborer; with him in the set, inequality increases by 50 per cent. One may charge that such a calculation is unjust: the farm laborer may only be working for a few years until he earns enough money to buy land further west; the son working on his father's farm may someday inherit the farm. The argument pushed to its extreme means that so long as there is any free land in America, then there is relative equality. This is similar to the claim that as long as there are jobs available somewhere, there is no unemployment. One must account for all of the individuals in a region at a given time.

The question of multiple ownership must also be dealt with. Table 30 gives the distribution of wealth in real estate and personal estate of farmers living in Milwaukee County in 1860. These individuals certainly might have owned land in other counties or owned more than one farm in Milwaukee County. This is contrasted to the previous Milwaukee distributions which pertained to values for individual farms in the county. The inequality coefficient for farmers of 0.725 is 15 per cent larger than our $R_{1+2} = 0.64$.

One might oversimplify the Milwaukee results by the following list:

Distribution of	Gini coefficient in Milwaukee County, 1860	Reason for the difference
Land acreage	0.38	Fertility, city proximity
Land value of farms	.44	
Land value of farms and zero values for farm laborers	.64	Farm laborers and farmers with no land
Wealth of farm population	.73	Multiple ownership including land in other counties

It is noted that our 0.725 (or 0.73) value for wealth distribution is still substantially less than that for the urban, or, more properly, the non-farmer distribution. The 0.725 coefficient happens to be the same as the wealth distribution of Wisconsin, excluding Milwaukee County, in 1860. The 0.725 value, however, was large in a country with available land in 1860 at $1.25 an acre.

This is not to deprecate the availability of free land. Obviously, many persons would not have come without it. It is perhaps not unfair at this juncture briefly to compare land inequality in Wisconsin with that in Great Britain at the same period, where inequality was considered to be greater than in France or Germany.[11] The data of Table 31 encompass the elements of multiple ownership and farm laborers. Surely inequality was larger. The value of R was 0.8 or 0.9 instead of 0.7. If one eliminates cottagers, then 400 peer and peeress landowners owned 16.6 per cent of 34.5 million acres of land in England and Wales. These 400 represented 0.157 per cent of landowners. In Milwaukee County in 1860, this per cent would represent 4 of the 2,680 individuals. The top 4 individuals had 8.4 per cent of the total wealth of farmers, not 16 per cent. Interesting, however, is the fact that gross revenues of the top 400 landowners in England and Ireland in 1874—75 from land were probably less than 10 per cent of total revenues. The difficulty with this formulation of the problem is that gross receipts are not strictly ordered from highest to lowest value. Some general statements might also be made about German ownership but it is difficult to evaluate the farm labor problem.[12]

In summary, it would seem that there was more inequality of land holdings in Milwaukee and Wisconsin than one might imagine would have existed in the middle of the last century. In terms of dollar value of holdings, inequality was approximately 20 per cent less than in rural England or in Milwaukee city. Evidence after 1870 leads to the conclusion that inequality of land acreage decreased at the same time that agricultural land drew a smaller and smaller portion of the total labor force.

The findings presented in earlier chapters based on the excellent data, particularly for 1860, were that wealth inequality was high in the early development of Wisconsin. Mortgage debt information for 1880—1889 and estate data for 1927 and 1962 lead to the conclusion that this level did not materially change in the last one hundred years among older persons in Wisconsin, especially among those who were affluent. The values for the Gini coefficient ranged from 0.65 to 0.75.

In the case of Milwaukee County, inequality in upper deciles apparently changed little from 1860 until the turn of the century, if estate data for 1900 may be used as a guide. There is some cogent appeal for feeling that lower- and middle-decile groups may have fared relatively well in acquiring wealth in the 30 years after 1860, based on 1870 wealth data and 1880—1889 mortgage debt figures. No concrete

Table 31. British Land Ownership, 1873—1875

England and Wales, 1873

Class	Number of owners	Acres (thousands)
Peers and Peeresses	400	5,728
Great Landowners	1,288	8,497
Squires	2,529	4,319
Greater Yeomen	9,585	4,782
Lesser Yeomen	24,412	4,144
Small proprietors	217,049	3,931
Cottagers	703,289	151
Public bodies	14,459	1,443
Waste	—	1,524
	973,011	34,523[a]

The concentration coefficient of private holders is 0.817 excluding cottagers and 0.944 including cottagers.

England and Ireland, 1874—75

Lower class limit (in acres)	Number of persons	Acreage (thousands)	Estimate of gross Revenues (£ 000)
100,000—	1	181	161
50,000—	3	194	188
20,000—	66	1,917	2,331
10,000—	223	3,098	4,337
5,000—	581	3,974	5,522
2,000—	1,815	5,529	9,579
1,000—	2,719	3,799	7,914
500—	4,799	3,317	6,427
100—	32,317	6,827	13,680
50—	25,839	1,791	4,302
10—	72,640	1,750	6,509
1—	121,983	478	6,438
0—	703,289	151	29,127
	966,275	33,006	96,515

The concentration coefficient for acreage was 0.858 for those holding 1 acre or more and 0.774 for those holding 10 acres or more. The concentration coefficients of gross revenues based on these same classifications were 0.697 and 0.678.

[a]Figures in this column do not add to total because of rounding.

Source: 1873, John Bateman, *The Great Land Owners of Great Britain and Ireland* (4th ed., London, 1883), this table is culled from *The Modern Domesday Book* and correspondence to correct for variation in spelling of names of landowners with holdings in several counties. Bateman suggests several changes above 2,000 acres showing greater concentration: (Lower class limit in acres—frequency) 100,000—44; 50,000—71; 20,000—299; 10,000—487; 6,000—617; 3,000—982; 2,000—1,320; 1874—75, Charles B. Spahr, *The Present Distribution of Wealth in the United States* (New York, 1893), p. 162, as taken from the Domesday Book for 1874—75.

distributions for the county have been found after this date. There is
some inkling that the wealth-income ratio of persons may have decreased in the 100 years, particularly in Milwaukee County, but va-
garies of definitional changes of wealth and estates make it advisable
not to stress this finding.

How can it be that wealth concentration did not increase in an age
of urbanization and industrialization? What is the modern counterpart
to owning a fifty-acre farm? The mortgage debt analysis indicated
that ownership of lots became important in urban areas. The inheritance mechanism was one where the elite fostered, at most, one of the
same absolute size among progeny while the population increased
greatly. Incorporation and manufacturing helped institutionalize
wealth and to pool economic vicissitudes. The phenomenon of or-
ganized financial institutions may have been partially responsible for
decreased inequality in crop-land holdings.

The young, who had less wealth, are not now such a large per cent
of the adult labor force. The foreign born, who had less wealth, have
now all but disappeared. The greatest leveller of all is education.
The concentration coefficient of the distribution of formal years of education among adults has decreased dramatically to less than half, perhaps one fourth of what it was 100 years ago.

Ultimately, however, the argument must rest on the fact that there
was such high inequality at the time of settlement until prior to the
Civil War. The relative difficulties in obtaining title to land, the need
for hired farm laborers, and the tremendous influx of the penniless
foreign born left a large element of the labor force propertyless at any
given point in time.

Chapter 7

Income Distribution in Milwaukee and Wisconsin

An investigation has been made of the wealth distribution in 1860 and 1870. Income distributions for intervening years in the decade may be obtained in part from income tax returns; those for 1864 will be used here. After this period, one can find no meaningful income data until 1913. There was an abortive income tax in the year 1894 with some fragmentary initial returns, but data were incomplete. With the advent of the Wisconsin state income tax law, one obtains the first income distribution available in 45 years, that for the year 1913. Milwaukee County distributions were published for 1913, 1929, 1934, 1935, and 1936. Wisconsin distributions were published for 1913, 1919, 1922–25, 1929, 1934, 1935, 1936, and 1949. Some unpublished distributions are available for other years. Data also exist for Wisconsin from federal income tax returns for most years since 1913. The census volumes of 1939 and 1949 contain wage distributions for Milwaukee and Wisconsin. The censuses of 1949 and 1959 contain income distributions.

The income tax data are incomplete for lower income groups. Filing requirements are usually lax or have a sufficiently high income requirement that many persons have not filed returns. This was particularly true before World War II. Only in the census of 1949 can there be found complete information about incomes of the lowest groups. Thus, an enumeration of all strata, a comprehensive picture, does not exist between the wealth distribution of 1860 and the income distributions of the late 1940's. Data from several sources must be pieced together in arriving at an understanding of what took place in the intervening years.

A. MILWAUKEE COUNTY INCOME

1. *Pareto Curves in 1864, 1929, and 1959.*

The incomes of higher-income persons in Milwaukee for each year from 1863 to 1868 were published in the *Milwaukee Sentinel*. The income tax records are now beginning to be made available by the National Archives and Records Service in Washington for all counties and tax districts in Wisconsin. We shall examine the Milwaukee County information for 1864, an income year with about the same relative dispersion as in other years. The filing requirement was lowest in real money terms in 1864; and 1,874 persons or 10 per cent of the interpolated 1860–1870 number of men declared incomes.[1]

1864 income lower-class limit, X	Cumulative number of persons, L_X
$100,000–	1
50,000–	4
10,000–	85
5,000–	186
1,000–	1,032
600–	1,874
0– (unreported cases = 16,326)	18,200

The 1864 data are plotted for 18 classes as an inverse-Pareto curve in Exhibit 21. Adjusted to 1860 prices, $X = aN_X^{-b}$ is $X = \$83\, N_X^{-0.711}$, $N = 18$, $0.000055 \le N_X \le 0.103$. One may begin by relating this to the comparable situation for the wealth distribution in Milwaukee County in 1860. Then $W = \$829 N_W^{-0.793}$, $N = 9$, $0.00020 \le N_X \le 0.102$. Wealth inequality of this top group was 10 per cent larger than income inequality as measured by the ratio of the two b values. The average income of the top group in 1860 dollars was $1,410 and the average wealth was $19,460. This seems reasonable in terms of rates of return, since the ratio of average income to average wealth was 7.2 per cent.

Two other income distributions, those for 1929 and 1959, have been chosen for comparison with that for 1864 because of the very revealing contrasts indicating economic growth and decreased inequality. These curves are portrayed in Exhibit 21 using 1860 prices with the following quantifications:

1929: $X = \$435\, N_X^{-0.567}$, $N = 17$, $0.00027 \le N_X \le 0.624$

1959: $X = \$1,104\, N_X^{-0.406}$, $N = 16$, $0.000045 \le N_X \le 0.789$.

Exhibit 21
Inverse Pareto Curves for Milwaukee in 1864, 1929, and 1959[a] (in 1860 Prices)

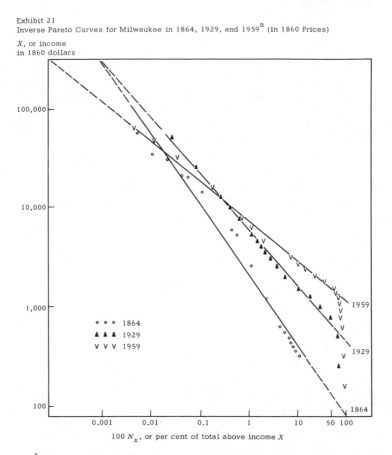

X, or income
in 1860 dollars

100 N_x, or per cent of total above income X

[a]Data are for males 14 years old and over with income, see U.S. Treasury Department, *Statistics of Income Tax Returns, 1959* (Washington, D.C., 1961), pp. 77–85, 94. The Milwaukee Standard Metropolitan Area returns above $10,000 (which account for almost exactly the same number as the census frequency above $10,000) and SMA returns for $7,000 to $10,000 are spliced into the basic returns. A similar procedure is used for Wisconsin. This technique increases the Gini coefficient slightly. For price indices, see Appendix 3.

Sources: 1864 data, *Milwaukee Sentinel*, 1865: Aug. 4, 5, 7; 1929 data, *Wisconsin Tax Commission, Wisconsin Individual Income Tax Statistics, 1929 Income* (n.p.; n.d.), pp. A2, A28; 1959 data, U.S. Bureau of the Census. 18th Census, 1960. Vol. 1, *Characteristics of the Population* (Washington, D.C., 1963), Part 51 (Wisconsin), pp. 197, 268–73.

We first examine the ramifications of extending these linear relationships in logarithms to $N_X = 1.00$, using our implied lower limits when $N_X = 1.00$ and the slopes of the lines in determining[2] $X = a/(1 - b)$:

	b	Implied lower limit (in 1860 dollars) a	Implied arithmetic mean (in 1860 dollars) $\overline{X}$
1864	0.711	83	287
1929	.568	435	1,008
1959	.406	1,104	1,859

Now very remarkable results occur when one computes the average annual per cent of change based on these implied means and the time intervals of 65 years, 30 years, and 95 years:

(Average annual per cent of change)

Years	1929	1959
1864	1.95	1.98
1929		2.05

The rates coincide with that obtained by fitting an exponential trend to decennial wage averages in manufacturing in Milwaukee in the last 100 years, where $Y = \$244(1.018)^t$, $t = 0$ in 1860 and Y = the rate in 1860 dollars. Data are in Appendices 3 and 4.

One might feel that 1.98 per cent is a little large, but it must be remembered that one is dealing with a dynamic county and with incomes of males. The averages are not swamped in the latter stages with females in lower income groups. It may still be maintained that the implied means are exaggerated. The implied value for 1959, for example, is 5.4 per cent larger than the actual arithmetic mean. This 5.4 per cent is the amount of income it would take to raise the incomes of lower income groups sufficiently to yield an effective Pareto curve for $0 \le N_X \le 1.000$. It is not known how much the 1929 implied average is exaggerated. There is the presumption of underfiling. If the 30 per cent of persons not accounted for had incomes only half that of the implied lower limit, it would mean the implied average was 7 per cent too high a figure. When inequality is large, the implied lower limit is a small per cent of average income. If the analysis is applied only to the top 50 per cent of persons, lower growth rates are obtained as expected:

	b as already obtained	Implied lower limit of top 50 per cent ($N_X = 0.50$; 1860 \$)	Implied arithmetic mean of top 50 per cent ($N_X = 0.50$; 1860 \$)
1864	0.711	136	471
1929	.568	645	1,490
1959	.406	1,464	2,460

(Average annual per cent of change)

Years	1929	1959
1864	1.80	1.76
1929		1.68

On the whole, the implied averages check remarkably well with the
known facts. One is not certain about 1864, but it can be shown, after
examining 1860 wage rate data with an average income of $264 for
Milwaukee County, that average income for 1864 in 1860 dollars was
reasonably close to the $287 value. It is on the strength of the growth
results from the three Pareto curves that one has much greater confidence in making inferences about inequality.[3]

It has been stated that the Pareto form $\log X = \log a - b \log N_X$ has
a concentration coefficient $R = b/(2 - b)$ for a continuous distribution.
For the Milwaukee data:

	b	Implied R	Actual R	Possible actual R
1864	0.711	0.551	—	0.654–0.750
1929	.568	.397	—	.500– .555
1959	.406	.255	0.358	—

The implied R in 1959 was 0.46 times that in 1864 and 0.64 times that
in 1929. The implied R value in 1959 of 0.255 for Milwaukee County
can also be compared to the actual R value of 0.358 in that year. This
disparity results from the difference of Lorenz curves for the lowest 30
to 35 per cent of recipients. The Lorenz curve for actual data goes
close to the base line while that from the Pareto line, with its implied
lower limit, does not. This phenomenon will be illustrated in Exhibit
23, depicting a Lorenz curve with the Pareto assumption. One is left
with the necessity of adjusting the implied R's in 1929 and 1864 for
the same discrepancy if he wishes some estimate of the actual R in
those two years. The most conservative policy would be to add the absolute difference, $0.358 - 0.255 = 0.103$ in 1959 to the R's in 1929 and
1864. This would lead to values of $0.397 + 0.103 = 0.500$ in 1929, and
$0.551 + 0.103 = 0.654$ in 1864. Alternatively, one might apply the ratio
$0.358/0.255$. This gives an R of 0.555 in 1929 and 0.750 in 1864.

It is of interest to study income changes considering the absolute
number of males in the labor force, L_X, who are above income X rather
than the per cent of persons, N_X, that are above X. The Pareto curve
may be adapted by substituting $L_X = N_X L_0$, where L_0 is the number
of cases in the labor force.

	L_0 for Milwaukee
1864	18,200
1929	233,800
1959	330,552

$$1864: \quad \log X = 4.9479 - 0.7109 \log L_X$$

$$1929: \quad \log X = 5.6906 - 0.5684 \log L_X$$

$$1959: \quad \log X = 5.2846 - 0.4061 \log L_X$$

These equations have been plotted in Exhibit 22. The values for the top man for these equations show an increase from 1864 to 1959. The implied top man's income in 1959 was more than two and one half times the top man's income in 1864. This is equivalent to an average annual change of 0.85 per cent. The remarkable thing is that it was a positive rate and sufficient to be not much less than half the 1.98 per cent average growth among males. The tenth man had an annual average increase of 1.5 per cent and the hundredth man an increase of 2.2 per cent per annum in the 95-year period. This was in the face of a large percentage loss for the top decile group as a whole. How can this happen?

The population increase is the camouflage. If population doubles, the top two persons must have an income averaging the same as that

Exhibit 22
The Number of Persons Related to Income, Obtained from Milwaukee Pareto Curves for 1864, 1929, and 1959 (in 1860 Prices)

X, or income of males at the rung L_X, in 1860 dollars

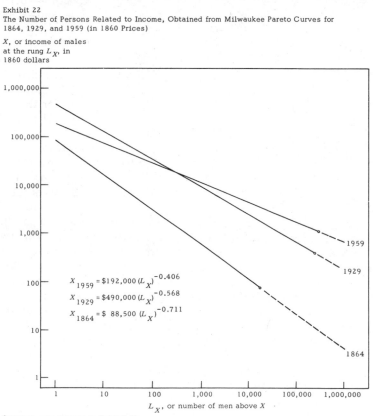

$$X_{1959} = \$192,000 \, (L_X)^{-0.406}$$
$$X_{1929} = \$490,000 \, (L_X)^{-0.568}$$
$$X_{1864} = \$ \, 88,500 \, (L_X)^{-0.711}$$

L_X, or number of men above X

Sources: see sources to Exhibit 21.

of the former top man for relative comparability. If one thinks of the top person in both periods as Mr. A, he may or may not consider that Mr. A. has suffered. In one sense it may be argued that the society twice as large must have doubled the leadership capacity it had and should pay A and B an average equivalent to A's former remuneration. In another sense, one says Mr. A must produce to stay on top and if he does, he will be rewarded. If one continues this reasoning to the 100th, 10,000th, or 1,000,000th man, he finds himself in the position of wondering what the Pareto curve would be like for hypothetical increases in population.

2. *Lorenz Curves in 1864 and 1929.*

The procedure used earlier for obtaining a Gini coefficient for Milwaukee in 1864 was to extend the inverse–Pareto curve below the $600 filing requirement until all cases had been absorbed. Two other possible procedures are to assume either a rectangular or a trapezoidal distribution below $600 ($340 in 1860 prices):

	Pareto	Rectangular	Trapezoidal
$600 and up	1,874	1,874	1,874
500–599	425	2,721	999
400–499	650	2,721	1,687
300–399	1,125	2,721	2,376
200–299	2,300	2,721	3,065
100–199	7,000	2,721	3,754
83– 99	4,826		
0– 99		2,721	4,443
	18,200	18,200	18,200
R	0.64	0.55	0.60

These are graphed as Lorenz curves in Exhibit 23 along with the 1959 Lorenz curves for males with an R of 0.358. Inequality under the most favorable conditions does not give a Gini coefficient of less than 0.552 in 1864. The evidence seems very strong in indicating substantial decreases in inequality during the century in Milwaukee County.

It is noted from the curves that it is the rich group and its income which starts the initial drop in the 1864 curve below that in 1959. It is the lower tail of the distribution in 1864 about which we are uncertain. Daily wage rates for carpenters and day laborers without board were analyzed by ward for Milwaukee in 1860, using the census manuscript reports. The lowest daylabor rate in the state was reported in one Milwaukee ward (40¢ using 1860 prices, or $1.33 using 1960 prices). Possible annual rates, assuming 200 to 300 days work in a year,[4] would range from $100 to $411 in 1860. Incomes of those newly arrived may

Exhibit 23
Lorenz Curves of Milwaukee Income in 1959, and Possible Lorenz Curves for
Milwaukee Income in 1864[a]

$\overline{A}_x$, or per cent
of income

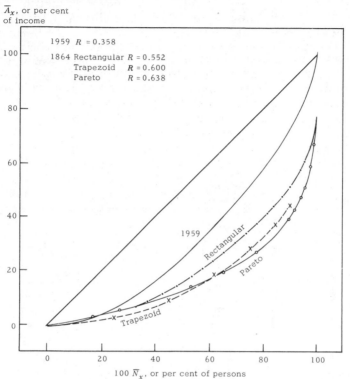

1959 R = 0.358

1864 Rectangular R = 0.552
     Trapezoid R = 0.600
     Pareto R = 0.638

1959

Rectangular

Pareto

Trapezoid

100 $\overline{N}_x$, or per cent of persons

[a]Data are for males 14 years old and over with income. See U.S. Treasury
Department, *Statistics of Income Tax Returns, 1959* (Washington, D.C., 1961),
pp. 77–85, 94. The Milwaukee Standard Metropolitan Area returns above $10,000
(which account for almost exactly the same number as the census frequency over
$10,000) and SMA returns for $7,000 to $10,000 are spliced into the basic returns.
This technique increases the Gini coefficient slightly.

Sources: 1864 data, *Milwaukee Sentinel*, 1865: Aug. 4, 5, 7; 1959 data, U.S.
Bureau of the Census. 18th Census, 1960. Vol. 1, *Characteristics of the Population* (Washington, D.C., 1963), Part 51 (Wisconsin), pp. 191, 268–73.

have been quite low. A study of day labor rates, Y_{DL}, and density, D,
in 1860 in 32 of Wisconsin's counties leaves: log Y_{DL} = 0.0923 –
0.0765 log D, N = 32, r^2 = –0.55. Day labor rates were indeed less in
the more densely populated areas.

B. WISCONSIN INCOME

Income tax returns are available from the National Archives for five
of the six tax districts of Wisconsin in 1864. The missing district was

of average size, judged on the basis of income tax receipts for that
year. The five districts reported 5,590 individuals with incomes above
$600 for the income year 1863. Their average income was $1,410. The
incomes were ranked from highest to lowest and found to conform
nicely to a Pareto curve. One obtains a $b = 0.58$ by fitting our formula
by the method of least squares to 17 points selected at even intervals
throughout the income range above $600. This value for the slope
should be compared to those in a later period of Wisconsin history.

It is possible to obtain a continuous series for Wisconsin inequality if one uses Bureau of Internal Revenue data since 1913. In Exhibit
24 are presented measures of inequality for 33 years from distributions
largely pertaining to both males and females.[5] If one fits a trend line
to the 33 inverse slopes above $2,000, he obtains an equation $b =
0.78 - 0.0035\, t$, where $t - 1860 = 0$. There is the problem that the per

Exhibit 24
Slopes[a] of Inverse Pareto Curves Obtained from Wisconsin Income Tax Returns,
Selected Years, 1916–1962

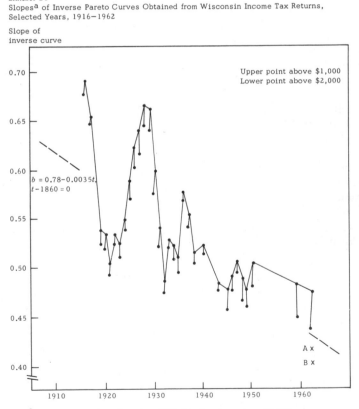

[a]A is the slope above $3,000 in 1962; B is the slope above $4,000.

Source: Bureau of Internal Revenue, *Statistics of Income, Individual Income Tax
Returns*, various issues.

cent of cases above $2,000 in a past year is much less than in a present year. Since a least-squares slope of the inverse Pareto type usually increases as one adds lower income classes, our trend would not adequately measure decreased inequality. Points A and B on the charts give some quantitative measures of this bias. It is not unreasonable to state that the inequality decrease in upper tail data in a period of nearly 50 years is at a rate easily sufficient to account for a halving of income inequality for a century. It is noted, however, that the trend value in 1900—1910 is similar to that for Wisconsin in 1863.

Again, one may claim that there is no concrete evidence of what occurred between 1864 and 1913, that a strong downward trend in the last 50 years may be a correction from increased inequality. But one does know that the backward extrapolation to 1900 yields a figure not dissimilar from the 1860 value as evidenced from the 1864 Wisconsin data. One does know that changes in nativity, age, education, class of worker, dependence on farm land, and real estate distribution were factors prevailing throughout the 100 years.

Data for 1913, 1919, 1929, and 1936 from the Wisconsin Tax Commission all give an inverse Pareto slope larger for Milwaukee than for Wisconsin. Not until after World War II does one find a value which is less. Gini coefficients of census data of 1949 and 1959 incomes are less for Milwaukee than for Wisconsin. It is quite conceivable, then, that it was not until after World War II that the inequality downtrend for Milwaukee passed underneath that for Wisconsin.

Finally, one might examine some specific groups today which might give indications of the inequality path. Exhibit 25 shows that the disparity between income inequality of males in rural farm and urban districts was 0.457—0.372 as measured by R from the 1959 data. Thus, rural districts have $0.457/(0.372) - 1 = 23$ per cent more inequality than urban areas and $0.457/(0.358) - 1 = 28$ per cent more inequality than in Milwaukee. One would expect lessening inequality in the future as the urban movement continues:

(Male population 20 years old and over)

	Milwaukee County	Wisconsin	Milwaukee County/ Wisconsin
1860	15,899	199,476	0.08
1910	141,000	706,558	0.20
1960	317,127	1,163,965	0.27

In the meantime one would expect Milwaukee's inequality to decrease, perhaps to the inequality of those working 52 weeks a year or to a homogeneous age group. Exhibit 25 gives illustrations of possible Pareto curves for these latter two groups. Their concentration coefficients are each about 0.26. But decreases in inequality might occur

Exhibit 25
Pareto Curves for Selected Groups of Males in Wisconsin and Milwaukee in 1959

X, or income
in dollars

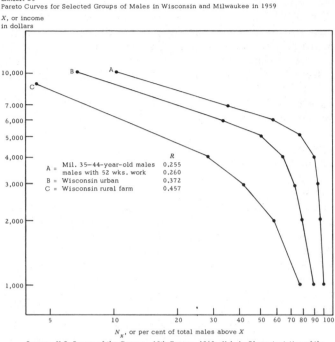

N_x, or per cent of total males above X

Source: U.S. Bureau of the Census. 18th Census, 1960. Vol. 1, *Characteristics of the
Population* (GPO: Washington, D.C., 1963), pp. 459, 460, 464.

even in these groups as there is full utilization of manpower resources.
If the lower tails of the Pareto curves were raised so that the men's
productivity fully followed the Pareto logarithmic configuration, the
concentration coefficient could decrease from 0.26 to 0.21. It would
seem the process is a continual one.

    An interpretation can be given of how decreased income inequality
has permeated society in the last 100 years in Milwaukee County and
at least the last 50 years in Wisconsin. The essential feature is that
middle-income groups have gained relative to the rich and the poor.
In earlier times, there was probably more of a continuous gradation in
income configurations in going from rich to poor. The rise of middle-
income groups has made the plight of the poor more glaring.

C. SUMMARY

    The materials of this supplementary chapter on income indicate that
income of men in Wisconsin is distributed less unequally now than it
was a century ago. The highest income subset does not have so large
a portion of the income aggregate as it did fifty or one hundred years
ago. Middle-income groups have fared much better, at least since

World War I; we are uncertain about low-income groups. It should be remembered that winter seasonal factors may have depressed annual incomes in the earlier period. Urban groups probably have experienced greater levelling of income than rural groups. The strongly urban area of Milwaukee County had an inequality coefficient of income somewhere between 0.55 and 0.75 in 1864. The coefficient was 0.35 in 1959, a figure less than that for the state as a whole in that year.

Is a finding of decreased income inequality inconsistent with the main wealth findings of this book? Let us review those aspects which are germane to this issue. Wealth inequality, particularly among upper-wealth groups, has changed very little in Wisconsin since its settlement. There is good evidence about the change for the rich, but not for the poor. Knowledge of wealth distribution in Wisconsin a century ago and in the United States today, coupled with some preliminary findings for the United States a century ago, lead one to feel that wealth inequality is about the same now as it was then.

How could income inequality decrease while wealth inequality remained constant? (This is a problem which the author has also found in studies of Norway.) There are many possible explanations. Private wealth may be relatively less important now in amount, or in the return it brings. Perhaps the private-wealth—private-income ratio has decreased substantially, in part because of increased wealth holdings by government. Perhaps the ratio has changed little, but income in the form of dividends, interest, and rent is now not so important relative to wages and salaries.[6] Certainly human wealth in the form of education is relatively more important and less unequally distributed.

There are many variables and institutional changes affecting the link between income and wealth as aggregates among all groups and among poor, average, and rich groups. These include saving and saving propensities, urbanity, aging, immigration, education, and intergenerational transfers of property to an expanding population. The study of wealth or income is a process without end.

The main thrust of this book has been one of understanding the quantitative and qualitative patterns of many factors as revealed by the wealth patterns in Wisconsin one hundred years ago. The overall findings of Chapter 1 uncover the marvelous regularity of an economic system which was a new and expanding one.

Appendix 1

Excerpts from Instructions to U.S. Marshals for the 1860 Census

In filling up this schedule, first enter on a sheet the pages, then fill up the blanks in the heading in their proper order, commencing with the less division, as town, township, ward, or borough; then the name of the county and State, with the date of taking; after that enter your own name and record the name of the post office of the vicinage. Every day you will change the date and on every page write your name. All the other entries are to be repeated so long as the returns apply, but the moment you enter upon another town, township, ward, borough, or county, you must change the heading to correspond. (Inasmuch as these directions are equally applicable to other schedules, as will appear on their face, they need not be repeated, although to be observed as if they were reiterated.)

1. *Dwelling houses numbered.*—Under heading 1, insert in numerical order the number of dwelling houses occupied by free inhabitants, as they are visited. The first house you enter is to be No. 1, the second, No. 2, and so on to the last house in your subdivision. The numbering of houses is to be continuously maintained, without regard to minor divisions, from the first to the last house included in your work, so that your last entry will express the whole number of dwelling houses in your subdivision. By "dwelling house" is meant a separate tenement, inhabited or uninhabited, and may contain one or more families under one roof. Where several tenements are in one block with walls to separate them having different entrances, they are each to be numbered separately, but where not so divided they are to be enumerated as one house. Houses which are tenentable but without inhabitants, are to be returned and numbered, but represented as unoccupied, in column 3, while no number is to be entered in column No. 2. If a house is used partly for a store or other purpose and partly for a dwelling, it is to

be numbered as a dwelling house. Hotels, poor houses, garrisons, hospitals, asylums, jails, penitentiaries, and establishments of kindred
character, are to be numbered, and if they consist of a group of several houses, each is to be numbered separately, while you will use
particular care to write longitudinally in the column the designation or
description of the house, and specify particularly and clearly whether
it or they be poor house, hotel, hospital, &c.

   2. *Families.*—Under heading 2, entitled "*Families numbered in
the order of visitation*," insert the number of families of free persons
as they are visited. By the term "family" is meant either one person
living separately and alone in a house, or a part of a house, and providing for him or herself, or several persons living together in a house,
or part of a house, upon one common means of support and separately
from others in similar circumstances. A widow living alone and separately providing for herself, or two hundred individuals living together
and provided for by a common head, should each be numbered as one
family. The resident inmates of a hotel, jail, garrison, hospital, or
other similar institution, should be recorded as one family, unless there
be several tenements or distinct families, in which case they should
be separated. There may be several families in a garrison, in which
case they should be recorded distinct, but should all, by a marginal
note, be embraced as of or belonging to such garrison.

   3. *Individual Names.*—Under heading 3, entitled "*The name of
every person whose usual place of abode on the 1st day of June, 1860,
was in this family*," insert the name of every free person in each family, of every age, including the names of those temporarily absent on
a journey, visit, or for the purposes of education, as well as those
that were at home on that day. The name of any member of a family who
may have died *since the 1st day of June* is to be entered and the person
described as if living, but the name of any person born since the 1st
day of June is to be omitted. The names are to be written beginning
with the father and mother, or if either or both be dead, begin with some
other ostensible head of the family, to be followed, as far as practic-
able, with the name of the oldest child residing at home, then the next
oldest, and so on to the youngest, then the other inmates, lodgers, and
boarders, laborers, domestics, and servants.

   All landlords, jailors, superintendents of poor-houses, garrisons,
hospitals, asylums, and other similar institutions, are to be considered
as heads of their respective families, and the inmates under their care
to be registered as members thereof, and the details concerning each,
designated in their proper columns, so distinctly as to preclude any
doubt as to who form the family proper and who the guests, prisoners,
or other inmates, carefully omitting all transient persons.

   4. By "place of abode" is meant the house or usual lodging place of
persons. Any one who is temporarily absent on a visit or journey, or
for other purposes, with the intention of again returning, is to be considered a member of the family to which he belongs, and not of that

where he may be temporarily sojourning; and care should be exercised
to make full inquiry for such absentees, that none may be omitted on
your lists whose names should properly appear there.

5. *Indians.*—Indians *not taxed* are not to be enumerated. The families of Indians who have renounced tribal rule, and who under State
or Territorial laws exercise the rights of citizens, are to be enumerated.
In all such cases write "Ind." opposite their names, in column 6, under
heading "Color."

6. *Eating-houses Stores, Shops, &c.*—You will make inquiry at
all stores, shops, eating-houses, and all similar places, and take the
name and description of every free person who usually slept there previous to or about the 1st day of June, provided such person be not
otherwise enumerated.

Ships and Vessels.—Persons on board any description of ships or
vessels accidentally or temporarily in port; those who are temporarily
boarding at a sailor's boarding or lodging-house, if they belong to
other places, are not to be enumerated in your district. All seafaring
people are to be enumerated at their land homes, or usual place of
abode, whether they be present or at sea; and if any free persons live
on vessels or boats, acknowledging no other home, they are to be enumerated as belonging to the place where they have been engaged,
shipped, or hired; and Assistants should make inquiry respecting all
vessels employed, in the internal navigation of the United States, and
thus enumerate all who are not recorded as belonging to some family
on shore; and all persons of such description, in any one vessel, are
to be considered as belonging to one family and the vessel as their
place of abode.

7. *Ages.*—Under heading 4, entitled *"Age,"* insert in figures what
was the specific age of each person at his or her last birth day previous to the 1st day of June, opposite the name of such person. Where
the exact age cannot be ascertained insert a number which shall be the
nearest approximation thereto. The exact or estimated age of every individual is to be recorded. If the person be a child under one year old,
born previous to the 1st day of June, the entry is to be made by the
fractional parts of a year, thus: one month, 1/12; two months, 2/12;
and so on to eleven months, 11/12. Omit months in all cases where
the person is of one year and upwards.

8. *Sex.*—Under heading 5, entitled *"Sex"* insert the letter "m" for
male, and "f" for female, opposite the name, in all cases, as the fact
may be.

9. *Color.*—Under heading 6, entitled *"Color,"* in all cases where
the person is white leave the space blank; in all cases where the person is black without admixture insert the letter "B;" if a mulatto, or of
mixed blood, write "M;" if an Indian, write "Ind." It is very desirable
to have these directions carefully observed.

10. *Profession, Trade, and Occupation.*—Under head 7, entitled
"Profession, occupation, or trade of each person over fifteen years

of age," insert the specific profession, occupation, or trade the individual being enumerated is reputed to follow. The proprietor of a farm for the time being, who pursues agriculture professionally or practically, is to be recorded as a farmer; *the men who are employed for wages by him are to be termed farm laborers.* The members, or inmates, of a family employed in domestic duties at wages you will record as "servants," or "serving," or "domestic," according to the custom of the vicinage. A mechanic who employs others under him is to be termed differently from the one employed. The first is a master mechanic, and should be termed "master mason," "master carpenter," &c., as the case may be, and you should be very particular in designating the employers or master mechanics from the workmen or employed. Where persons (over 15) are learning trades, or serving apprenticeship, they should be recorded as "apprentices," with the name of the trade whereunto they are apprenticed. The employment of every person over 15, having an occupation, should be asked and recorded. In *every case* insert the kind of labor and nature of apprenticeship.

When the individual is a clergyman, insert the initials of the denomination to which he belongs—as Meth. for Methodist; R.C. for Roman Catholic; O.S.P., Old School Presbyterian; P.E., Protestant Episcopal;—or other appropriate designation, as the case may require. If a person follows several occupations, insert the name of the most prominent. If the person should be a teacher or professor, state the character of the occupation, as teacher of French, of common school; professor of mathematics, of languages, of philosophy, &c. In fine, record the occupation of every human being, male and female, (over 15,) who has an occupation or means of living, and let your record be so clear as to leave no doubt on the subject.

12. *Value of Real Estate.*—Under heading 8, insert the value of real estate owned by each individual enumerated. You are to obtain this information by personal inquiry of each head of a family, and are to insert the amount in dollars, be the estate located where it may. You are not to consider any question of lien or encumbrance; it is simply your duty to enter the value as given by the respondent.

13. *Value of Personal Estate.*—Under heading 9, insert (in dollars) the value of personal property or estate. Here you are to include the value of all the property, possessions, or wealth of each individual which is not embraced in the column previous, consist of what it may; the value of bonds, mortgages, notes, slaves, live stock, plate, jewels, or furniture; in fine, the value of whatever constitutes the personal wealth of individuals. Exact accuracy may not be arrived at, but all persons should be encouraged to give a near and prompt estimate for your information. Should any respondent manifest hesitation or unwillingness to make a free reply on this or any other subject, you will direct attention to Nos. 6 and 13 of your general instructions and the 15th section of the law.

14. *Birth Place.*—Under heading 10, you are to insert the place of birth of every individual whose name you record. If born in the State or Territory of their present residence, insert the name, abbreviation, or initials of such State or Territory. If born out of the United States, insert the name of the country of birth. To insert simply Germany would not be deemed a sufficiently specific localization of birth place, unless no better can be had. The particular German State should be given—as Baden, Bavaria, Hanover. Where the birth place cannot be ascertained, write "unknown" in the proper column; but it must be of rare occurrence that the place of birth may not be understood. You should ascertain the exact birth place of children as well as of parents, and not infer because parents were born in Baden that so also were the children.

Appendix 2

Wealthholdings of Members of the Wisconsin State Senate in 1860

In Chapter 2 some emphasis was placed on the activities of the men of wealth in Milwaukee County. Little is known about this subject for Wisconsin as a whole because of the effort that would be required in examining records of many counties. One source of collected information is that of members of the Wisconsin State Senate in 1860. This allows an analysis of the importance of wealth in the political arena. What was the extent of wealth holdings of this group? How much did its wealth differ from that of the populace as a whole? Was there a difference in wealth among senators classified by political party? What was the relative importance of wealth as compared to that of other variables in the determination of political party affiliation of senators?

There were 31 members, including the President of the Senate, with only 3 not native born. A thorough search was made for each of these individuals in the census rolls of the various counties. It was possible to identify 27 of these individuals and thus obtain their wealth declarations. These are given for each individual in Table 32 and may be summarized as:

	Total	Republicans	Democrats
Number of men	27	15	12
Average age	40.7	43.5	37.0
Wealth average			
Arithmetic mean	$13,500	$16,600	$9,540
Median	$ 6,500	$ 6,500	$5,900

These wealth averages are considerably above those of adult males for the whole State. The elaborate stratified sample of the 199,451

Table 32. Data on Selected Members, Wisconsin State Senate, 1860

Name	Place of birth	Age	Years in Wis.	Political Party	Wealth in $
D. F. Bartlett	United States	36	14	Rep.	Unknown
A. I. Bennett	New York	52	7	Rep.	Unknown
Geo. Bennett	Connecticut	57	21	Rep.	12,000
Z. P. Burdick	New York	53	10	Rep.	5,590
Cicero Comstock	Ohio	43	15	Rep.	103,000
E. B. Cox	New York	50	10	Rep.	31,000
H. W. Curtis	New York	43	7	Rep.	3,500
Moses Davis	Vermont	39	5	Rep.	4,000
Edward Decker	Maine	33	14	Dem.	20,800
M. J. Egan	Ireland	32	2	Dem.	2,200
W. D. Fratt	New York	35	16	Dem.	17,500
Benj. Ferguson	Maine	40	16	Dem.	Unknown
Chas. R. Gill	New York	29	5	Dem.	3,500
Luther Hanchett	Ohio	34	10	Rep.	6,000
Fred Hilgen	Alderburg	54	16	Dem.	21,000
R. H. Hotchkiss	New York	40	23	Dem.	1,700
Buel Hutchinson	New York	30	11	Rep.	4,800
E. D. Masters	New York	43	26	Rep.	6,800
Densmore Maxon	New York	39	16	Dem.	6,800
B. G. Noble	New York	44	5	Rep.	300
E. L. Phillips	New York	52	7	Rep.	Unknown
Chas. G. Rodolf	Switzerland	41	25	Dem.	16,600
M. W. Seely	New York	44	11	Rep.	6,500
P. B. Simpson	Ohio	38	16	Dem.	5,000
J. W. Stewart	Ohio	37	19	Rep.	22,000
John B. Sweat	Vermont	32	17	Dem.	3,000
W. R. Taylor	Connecticut	39	10	Dem.	16,400
Samuel H. Thurber	New York	33	4	Dem.	—
G. W. Washburn	Maine	36	12	Rep.	20,000
D. Worthington	Connecticut	53	12	Rep.	3,500
N. H. Virgin	Pennsylvania	47	25	Rep.	20,000

Source: Schedule 1 of the 1860 Census of Population; L. H. D. Crane, *A Manual of Customs, Precedents, and Forms in Use in the Assembly of Wisconsin* (1860).

adult males 20 years old and over in Wisconsin in 1860 presented in Chapter 2 gives an arithmetic mean wealth of $1,450 and a median wealth of $425. The average state senator thus was 9.3 times as wealthy as the average adult, from the standpoint of the mean, and 15.3 times as wealthy, from the standpoint of the median. The comparison is somewhat misleading. One should perhaps consider age-nativity classifications. In general, the average adult male in Wisconsin in 1860 was younger and much more likely to be foreign born. A better idea of the economic position of senators in Wisconsin may be obtained by considering these factors.

A study was made of approximately 50 per cent of adult males 40 years old in Wisconsin in 1860, yielding the following results:

Average Wealth of Adults 40 Years of Age in Wisconsin in 1860

Nativity	Number	Arithmetic mean wealth	Median wealth
Native born	1,457	$3,015	$1,200
Foreign born	2,903	1,190	500
Total	*4,360*	*1,800*	*610*

Source: 1860 Census of Population. This sample was obtained by taking all 40-year old males listed on the left-hand pages of the bound volumes. The sample is described much more fully in Chapter 5.

One sees that whereas only one third of the state's male adults in the senatorial age range were native born, 28 of the 31 senators were native born. The wealth averages for senators were 4.5 to 5.5 times those for native-born males who were 40 years old. The wealth averages of these native-born 40-year-olds are dominated by Yankees since 84 per cent were born in New England or the Middle Atlantic States. The senators were not only Yankees, they were rich Yankees having wealth 5 times that of other Yankees of the same age.

A multiple regression analysis can be made of the data for the senators in examining wealth, age, and residence by using the method of least squares. Letting W be wealth in 1860, and A be age in 1860, we have:[1]

$$\log W = 2.7529 + 0.0270\,A, \text{ where } n = 27, R = 0.33 \text{ and}$$
$$(0.0156)$$
$$W = \$566\,(1.064)^{A}.$$

It is seen that, on the average, a senator one year older than another had 6.4 per cent more wealth. This figure is quite consistent with two other studies, one of individual adult males in Milwaukee County and one of the 58 county aggregates in 1860. Senatorial representation was consistent with that of the population in the sense of reflecting the dynamics of private wealth accumulation through time. The fact that the Democratic members had less wealth than the Republican members could almost be attributed to age and to this dynamic alone. The 6.5 years age differential at 6.4 per cent a year leads to the calculation $\$9,540\,(1.064)^{6.5} = \$9,540\,(1.5) = \$14,300$. This age-adjusted average of $14,300 is much closer to that of the Republican average of $16,600. One almost obtains a figure for wealth by picking an age group.

Another variable, not elsewhere available for studies of Wisconsin residents, may be introduced in our analysis of senators. The number of years that each of the individuals had been in Wisconsin averaged 13.3. If this variable, Y, is introduced in the regression analysis:

$$\log W = 3.3159 + 0.0402 \ Y, \text{ where } n = 27, \ R = 0.43.$$
$$(0.0166)$$
$$W = \$2,070 \ (1.097)^Y.$$

$$\log W = 2.6273 + 0.0188 \ A + 0.0346 \ Y, \text{ where } n = 27, \ R = 0.51.$$
$$(0.0153) \qquad (0.0171)$$
$$W = \$424 \ (1.044)^A \ (1.083)^Y.$$

The variables Y and A are correlated, of course, but not unduly so. Age now has a net effect of 4.4 per cent a year while residence has a strong effect of 8.3 per cent a year. Thus for two people of the same age, the one in Wisconsin a year longer than the other had 8.3 per cent more wealth.

We may consider our variables W, A, and Y as predictors of political party, P, where $P = 1$ if the individual was a Republican and 0 if the individual was a Democrat:

$$P = -0.8787 + 0.0279 \ A - 0.0170 \ Y + 0.1363 \ \log W,$$
$$(0.0128) \qquad (0.0151) \qquad (0.1663)$$
where $n = 27$, $R = 0.43$.

In interpreting the results, one can first focus on the variable A. If one person was 10 years older than another but otherwise had the same length of residence and wealth as the other, he was on the average 0.0279×10, or 0.28, of the distance from $P = 0$ to $P = 1$. We can say this age differential increases his chances of being a Republican by 27.9 per cent. Likewise, a person 10 years longer in the state had a 17 per cent greater probability of being a Democrat. A person with 10 times as much wealth as another had a 13 per cent greater probability of being a Republican.

Certainly the coefficients associated with age and wealth seem reasonable. Age and wealth were positively related with being a Republican. Why there was a negative coefficient associated with years of residence, Y, is difficult to visualize. It cannot be all attributed to netting out the effects of age and wealth since the simple regression of P and Y also had a negative coefficient. Perhaps Y was a proxy for memory, memory of some not too distant Republican legislature. Perhaps Y was a proxy for state and local problems transcending national problems since length of residence among these predominantly native-born persons should have been proportional to Wisconsin interests on the eve of the Civil War.

An intriguing question is whether age, length of residence, or wealth was the more important determinant. It is really impossible to answer the question since the three variables were interrelated, particularly wealth with age and residence. The simplest procedure may be to consider deciles among the 27 and apply them to our last-stated equation:

	_A_	_Y_	log _W_	_W_
1st decile	33 years	5 years	3.2304	$ 1,700
9th decile	53 years	25 years	4.3424	$22,000
decile range	20	20	1.1120	

Regression coefficients
from equation above   +0.0279   −0.0170   +0.1363

Regression coefficient
times the decile range   +0.5580   −0.3400   +0.1515

In a statistical sense, the decile range for age has twice as much more bearing (+0.55) on political party affiliation than length of residence (−0.34) and wealth (+0.15). One might assert that the age factor was as important as the residence and wealth factors in the determination of political affiliation. It must not be forgotten that the singling out of age meant the singling out of wealth in this dynamic economy. Nevertheless, wealth was much less of a factor in distinguishing Republican from Democratic senators than it was in distinguishing senators from non-senators.

Appendix 3

Consumer Price Index, 1840–1963

Year	Index	Year	Index	Year	Index
1840	98	1874	129	1898	94
1850	90	1875	123	1899	94
1851	92	1876	119	1900	95
1852	93	1877	118	1901	96
1853	93	1878	111	1902	97
1854	101	1879	108	1903	100
1855	104	1880	110	1904	101
1856	102	1881	111	1905	101
1857	105	1882	112	1906	102
1858	99	1883	107	1907	106
1859	100	1884	104	1908	104
1860	100	1885	102	1909	103
1861	101	1886	102	1910	108
1862	113	1887	102	1911	108
1863	139	1888	104	1912	110
1864	176	1889	104	1913	112
1865	175	1890	103	1914	114
1866	167	1891	104	1915	115
1867	157	1892	103	1916	123
1868	154	1893	102	1917	145
1869	147	1894	97	1918	170
1870	141	1895	95	1919	196
1871	135	1896	95	1920	227
1872	135	1897	94	1921	202
1873	133				

(continued)

(continued)

Year	Index	Year	Index	Year	Index
1922	190	1938	160	1953	303
1923	193	1939	157	1954	304
1924	194	1940	159	1955	303
1925	199	1941	167	1956	308
1926	200	1942	185	1957	318
1927	196	1943	196	1958	327
1928	194	1944	199	1959	329
1929	194	1945	204		
		1946	221	1960	335
1930	189	1947	253	1961	338
1931	172	1948	272	1962	342
1932	155	1949	270	1963	346
1933	146			1964	351
1934	151	1950	272	1965	356
1935	155	1951	294	1966	367
1936	157	1952	301	1967	377
1937	163			1968	394

[a]1860 = 100.

Source: 1840, 1850, and 1860, the Federal Reserve Bank of New York cost of living index, in U.S. Bureau of the Census, *Historical Statistics of the United States, Colonial Times to 1957* (GPO: Washington, D.C., 1960), p. 127; 1860 to 1913, Ethel D. Hoover, "Retail Prices After 1850," in National Bureau of Economic Research, *Trends in the American Economy in the Nineteenth Century*, ed. William N. Parker, vol. 24, *Studies in Income and Wealth* (Princeton, N.J., 1960), pp. 142, 143, 162; 1913 to 1963, Bureau of Labor Statistics, Consumer Price Index, *Historical Statistics*, pp. 125, 126, and various issues of the *Monthly Labor Review*.

Appendix 4

Selected Time Series of Population and Production, Milwaukee County and Wisconsin, 1850–1960

	Population					Manufacturing			
Year	Total pop.	Male pop.	Male pop. 20 years old and over	Male pop. 21 years old and over	Year	No. of estab-lish-ments	Ave. no of wage earners	Total wages in mil-lions of dollars	Ave. wages in current dollars
				Milwaukee County					
1830	—								
1840	5,605	3,100	1,756		1840				
1850	31,077	16,410	8,812		1850	233	1,583		
1860	62,518	31,474	15,899	15,458	1860	558	3,406	0.90	264
1870	89,930	45,016	22,460	21,900	1870	828	8,433	3.40	404
1880	138,537	69,606		35,569	1880	886	21,318	7.08	333
1890	236,101	117,985		62,006	1890	2,917	43,829	20.83	482
1900	330,017	164,989		88,968	1900	3,523	53,530	22.58	427
1910	433,187	222,646		132,947					
1920	539,449	272,667		170,355	1919	2,247	106,137	117.6	1,108
1930	725,263	366,338	241,638	235,807	1929	1,939	117,658	170.9	1,453
1940	766,885	379,410	261,949	256,221	1939	1,657	80,255	112.0	1,396
1950	871,047	427,674	297,303	291,875	1947	1,963	177,702	535.0	3,011
1960	1,036,041	506,741	317,127	311,821	1954	1,979	175,802	809.8	4,602
				Wisconsin					
1830									
1840	30,945	18,757	11,690						
1850	305,391	164,716	84,479		1850	1,262	6,089	1.71	
1860	775,881	407,449	199,476		1860	3,064	15,414	4.27	277
1870	1,054,670	544,886	263,900	255,159	1870	7,013	43,910	13.58	309
1880	1,315,497	680,069	354,521	340,482	1880	7,674	57,109	13.81	242
1890	1,693,330	874,951	477,368	461,722	1890	10,417	120,006	42.96	358

(continued)

(continued)

| | Population | | | | | Manufacturing | | | |
Year	Total pop.	Male pop.	Male pop. 20 years old and over	Male pop. 21 years old and over	Year	No. of estab-lish-ments	Ave. no. of wage earners	Total wages in mil-lions of dollars	Ave. wages in current dollars
1900	2,069,042		589,641	570,615	1900	16,187	142,076	58.41	411
1910	2,333,860	1,208,578	706,558	683,743	1909	9,721	204,870	119.6	583
1920	2,632,067	1,356,718	821,907		1919	9,720	307,955	375.7	1,219
1930	2,939,006	1,510,815	942,477		1929	7,431	309,397	467.5	1,511
1940	3,137,587	1,60C,176	1,057,029		1939	6,354	250,774	364.5	1,447
1950	3,434,575	1,704,895	1,111,230		1947	6,980	418,674	1,190.8	2,844
1960	3,952,485	1,964,318	1,143,965		1954	7,702	429,919	1,814.3	4,220
					1958	7,793	428,735	2,139.4	4,990

Source: Schedule 1, 1860 and 1870 censuses; U.S. Censuses, selected years; U.S. Census Office. *Census Reports*, Vol. VIII, *Manufacturing*. Part II, *States and Territories* (GPO: Washington, D.C., 1902), p. 988; U.S. Bureau of the Census, *U.S. Census of Manufactures, 1958*, Vol. III, *Area Statistics* (GPO: Washington, D.C., 1961), pp. 48—5 (Wisconsin).

Notes

PREFACE

1   U.S. Bureau of the Census. 18th Census, 1960. Vol. I, *Characteristics of the Population* (GPO: Washington, D.C., 1963), Part
51, Wisconsin, p. 9.

CHAPTER 1

1   Lee Soltow, "Long-Run Changes in British Income Inequality,"
Economic History Review (April, 1968).
2   G. P. Watkins, "The Growth of Large Fortunes," *Publications of the
American Economic Association*, Third Series, 8 (1907); Carroll
D. Wright, "Are the Rich Growing Richer and the Poor Poorer?"
Atlantic Monthly, 80 (1897); Mathew Josephson, *The Robber
Barons* (New York, 1934); Robert Lampman, *The Share of Top
Wealth-Holders in National Wealth* (Princeton, 1962); C. A. and
M. R. Beard, *The Rise of American Civilization*, Vol. II, *The In-
dustrial Era* (New York, 1947); Merle Curti, *The Growth of American Thought* (New York, 1951) and Curti, *The Making of an American Community* (Stanford, 1959); Allan G. Bogue, *From Prairie
to Corn Belt* (Chicago, 1963); Paul W. Gates, *The Farmer's Age*
(New York, 1960); Joseph Schafer, *Four Wisconsin Counties* (Madison, 1927); Richard T. Ely, *Property and Contract in their Relation to the Distribution of Wealth* (New York, 1914); and E. A. Ross,
Social Control (New York, 1901).
3   See Appendix A for instructions to census enumerators.
4   As cited in the U.S. Bureau of the Census, *Historical Statistics of
the United States, Colonial Times to 1957* (GPO: Washington,
D.C., 1960), pp. 150, 151, 152.
5   A measure of relative dispersion, Gini's coefficient of concentration is calculated by determining the area between the actual
Lorenz curve and the straight-line curve of perfect equality. This
area as a ratio of the triangular area under the line of perfect

equality was 0.75 for Wisconsin in 1860. Values of the coefficient for perfect equality and perfect inequality are 0.0 and 1.0. An alternative interpretation of R is that it is the ratio of the average or mean difference to twice the mean. For the above data, the average difference between the wealth value of any individual and any other individual is $2,250; and R is $2,250/(2 \times $1,500)$, or 0.75.

6   Lampman, *Share of Top Wealth-Holders*, p. 228.

7   Dorothy S. Projector and Gertrude S. Weiss, *Survey of Financial Characteristics of Consumers*, Federal Reserve Technical Papers (Washington, 1966), pp. 110, 151.

8   The 1850 census did not use the term farm laborer. If it had, the proportion in farming in 1850 might very well have been larger than that in 1860.

9   Examples of Pareto charts are given in Exhibits 16 and 19. Suppose A = $100,000, b = 0.5, and $W = A(L_W)^{-b} = $100,000(L_W)^{-0.5}$. Then $L_{$100,000} = 1$; $L_{$10,000} = 100$; and $L_{$1,000} = 10,000$. Logarithms are used rather extensively in testing whether or not a Pareto curve is appropriate. This is because the Pareto formula appears as a straight line when logarithms are used. If $W = A(L_W)^{-b}$, then $\log W = \log A - b \log L_W$. It is noted that the three points in our example for $b = 0.5$ have $\log L_W$ of 0, 2, and 4 when $\log W$ is 5, 4, and 3. The slope b is, in effect, an elasticity coefficient E_{W,L_W} expressing percentage changes in wealth levels to percentage changes in the number of persons above these levels. One unacquainted with logarithms, Pareto curves, and demand curves with constant elasticity, might wish to see Gerhard Tintner, *Mathematics and Statistics for Economists* (New York, 1964), pp. 37—42.

CHAPTER 2

1   The census enumeration of 1860 was conducted from June 1 of that year. Oaths shown in the schedules indicate that the work of most assistant marshals was completed by August. There was some difficulty in the South. Mississippi had a few reports signed in December and schedules for three counties never reached Washington.

2   The 1860 instructions were obtained from the American Philosophical Society Library, Philadelphia. I am indebted to Professor Robert Gallman for telling me of their existence. The 1850 and 1870 instructions are from Carroll Wright and William Hunt, *History and Growth of the United States Census, 1790—1890* (Washington, 1900), pp. 152, 157. These authors found no 1860 instructions extant. Gallman is the author of the pioneer effort in sampling from the 1860 census. See Robert Gallman, "Trends in the Size Distribution of Wealth in the Nineteenth Century: Some Speculations," in National Bureau of Economic Research, *Six Papers on the Size Distribution of Wealth and Income*, ed. Lee Soltow, vol. 33, *Studies in Income and Wealth* (Princeton, N.J., 1969).

3   Works Progress Administration, *Annals of Cleveland, 1860*, 97
    vols. (Cleveland, 1937 [Multigraph]), Vol. 43, pp. 37—39.
4   See Joseph Schafer, *Four Wisconsin Counties* (Madison, 1927).
5   Lee Soltow, "The Share of Lower Income Groups in Income," *The
    Review of Economics and Statistics* (Nov., 1965).
6   Gerald J. Glasser, "Variance Formulas for the Mean Difference and
    Coefficient of Concentration," *Journal of the American Statistical
    Association* (Sept., 1962). If one has a lognormal distribution,
    s_X/μ is about the same as given in the table for R of 0.2 and 0.5;
    it is twice the value given in the table for $R = 0.8$. See J. Aitchison
    and J. A. C. Brown, *The Lognormal Distribution* (Cambridge, Eng.,
    1969), pp. 154—55.
7   The 1860 data include valuations for the 3,953,760 slaves. These
    appear largely in the personal property figures, except in Louisi-
    ana. If these persons are valued at $500 (suggested by David
    Wells, in *Our Burden and Our Strength* [Loyal Publication Society:
    London, 1864]), we have a value of $2 billion. The author has in-
    vestigated Mississippi valuations and has found an average value
    of from $800 to $900. If the 1,372,000 male and female slaves 20
    years old and over were valued at $1,000, we have a total estimate
    of $1.7 billion, not considering the value of children.
8   U.S. Bureau of the Census, *Historical Statistics of the United
    States, Colonial Times to 1957* (GPO: Washington, D.C., 1960),
    p. 147.
9   Ibid., pp. 150, 151, 152
10 Richard A. Easterlin, "Interregional Differences in Per Capita In-
    come, Population, and Total Income, 1840—1950," in National
    Bureau of Economic Research, *Studies in Income and Wealth*, Vol.
    24 (Princeton, N.J., 1960).
11 Schafer, *Four Wisconsin Counties*, p. 124.
12 State Historical Society of Wisconsin, *Dictionary of Wisconsin
    Biography* (Madison, 1960), pp. 205, 209, 210, 256; and Bayrd
    Still, *Milwaukee: The History of a City* (Madison, 1948), pp. 36,
    51, 58—60, 144, 155—56, 159, 170—73, 177—78, 182, 194, 196, 225,
    234, 247—49, 251, 327, 336, 355, 362, 392, 567.
13 U.S. Census Office. 8th Census, 1860. *Statistics of the United
    States (Including Mortality, Property, &c.,) in 1860* (GPO: Wash-
    ington, D.C., 1866), p. 330.
14 Freeman Hunt, *Worth and Wealth, a Collection of Maxims, Morals,
    and Miscellanies for Merchants and Men of Business* (New York,
    1856), p. 45.
15 In Norway, the institution of transferring a farm to the eldest son
    in exchange for food, clothing, and shelter until death was very
    highly developed in Law. Kjeld Helland-Hansen, Statsarkivar of
    Kristiansand, Norway, has made an elaborate study of the institu-
    tion.
16 Raymond W. Goldsmith, "The Growth of Reproducible Wealth of the
    United States of America from 1805 to 1950," International Associa-

tion for Research in Income and Wealth, *Income and Wealth of the United States: Trends and Structure*, Income and Wealth Series II (Cambridge, 1952), p. 306.

17   Of some little help were the *Dictionary of Wisconsin Biography* and some Works Progress Administration files of biography kept in the State Historical Library. The two genealogies are P. K. Kilbourn, *The History and Antiquities of the Name and Family of Kilbourn* (1856), and S. F. Kneeland, *Seven Centuries in the Kneeland Family* (New York, 1897).

18   In the Kilbourn line, the 1650 estate of the wife of Thomas was £335, net. Assuming there were 3 or 4 children, one might say there was £100 for each child. (Prices in England in 1660 differed little from those in 1860 as given in B. R. Mitchell, *Abstract of British Historical Statistics* [Cambridge, 1962], pp. 468—72.)

CHAPTER 3

1   The occupational census of 1860 for Wisconsin lists 93,859 as farmers and 31,472 as farm laborers, for a total of 125,331. This exceeds the theoretical number of $(0.598)(199,476) \doteq 119,000$ of Tables 6, 7, and 8.

2   If in some way one might eliminate the propertyless by giving farmers land or by giving non-farmers lots, inequality might be cut by 10 to 15 per cent. This could be accomplished over a period of time as the increased population of settlers tapered off and one did not continually have the oncoming rush of the propertyless.

3   The correlation coefficient $\overline{W}$ stratified sample mean and
                                                  for the county
$\overline{W}_{VEOI}$ averaged is 0.976 for $N = 58$.
     for the county

4   The wage data are given in part in Table 11. Burnette, Dallas, and Douglas counties have not been included. There were less than 10 adult males each in Dallas and Burnette.

5   It is appealing to point out that present income inequality among states is almost exactly half of the 0.19 value when computed in the same fashion as described above. This is also true when one investigates 1959 average income by county in Wisconsin.

6   Land Economics Institute, *Modern Land Policy* (Urbana, 1960), p. 86.

7   U.S. Department of Agriculture, *The Yearbook of Agriculture, 1957* (Washington, D.C., 1958), pp. 547—51. I could find no adequate data which would indicate the variation in the value of farm production due to soil conditions alone. In Lafayette County in the southern part of the state, the Gini coefficient in yields from one year to the next and between different areas in the county in a particular year is about 0.10. See also, Department of Agriculture,

Soil Survey of Lafayette County, Wisconsin, pp. 27, 71—73. If corn were grown on all land which produced at least 32 bushels per acre in the county, soil types would produce an $\bar{X}$ of 53.0 bushels with an R of 0.077. If one assumed that it was necessary to grow at least 30 bushels to break even, we could think of R as increasing to $(0.077)(53.0)/(53.0-30) = 0.178$. See also, U.S. Department of Agriculture, *Soil Survey of Barron County, Wisconsin*.

CHAPTER 4

1   The census enumeration apparently began on June 1 of each census year. Often assistant marshals submitted their enumerations dated August or September, sometimes later. G. H. Moore gives peak and trough, or downturn, dates of business cycles as: June, 1857, to Dec., 1858; Oct., 1860, to June, 1861; April, 1865, to Dec., 1867; June, 1869, to Dec., 1870; and Oct., 1873, to Mar., 1879 *(Statistical Indicators of Cyclical Revivals and Recessions* [New York, 1950], p. 6). The Cleveland Trust Index of American Business activity shows a cyclical position in the middle of 1870 similar to that in the middle of 1860. It is difficult to know how much conditions in a given year determined the wealth values declared by individuals. It is agreed that 1860 was the year of the greatest wheat crop in Wisconsin history. The price had been high in 1859 and probably dropped in 1860 after the census of 1860 was nearly completed. See Alan G. Bogue, *From Prairie to Corn Belt* (Chicago, 1963), p. 285.

2   Let VEOA be the value of the estate in the county as determined by assessors and reported in Schedule 6 of the 1850 Census, and let VEOT be the "true" value of the estate in the county as determined by an expert or by the assistant marshal and reported in the same Schedule. The real, personal, and total for VEOA and the total for VEOT for the state in 1850 were (in millions of dollars): 22.46, 4.26, 26.72, and 42.06. Real estate was 0.840 times total estate among VEOA figures. See U.S. Census Office. 7th Census, 1850. *Compendium* (GPO: Washington, D.C., 1854), p. 190.

3   See Benjamin Hibbard, *A History of the Public Land Policies* (Madison, 1965), esp. pp. 98, 147—48, 151, 155—56, 157, 158, 160, 162, 167, 379, 385.

4   Ibid., p. 158.

5   Ibid., p. 167. Professor Hibbard believed that this was not an indication of poor men being unable to pay for land they pre-empted, but one of speculation.

CHAPTER 5

1   Much of the following discussion about Kristiansand is based on

materials in Lee Soltow, *Toward Income Equality in Norway* (Madison, 1965).

2   The Milwaukee income data were described briefly in the summary of Chapter 1. They will be elaborated at greater length in the income supplement, Chapter 7.

3   Theodore Blegen, *Norwegian Migration to America 1825—1860* (Northfield, 1931).

4   Correspondence with the director of the Statistisk Sentralbyraa, Oslo. A *riksdaler* and a *speciedaler* were interchangeable.

5   Schedules 5 and 6 of the 1850, 1860, and 1870 Censuses of the United States; Central Bureau of Statistics of Norway, *Statistical Survey, 1948*, Norges Offisielle Statistikk. X: 178.

6   Blegen, *Norwegian Migration*, p. 313.

7   Ibid., map, p. 77. See also Margaret Snyder, *The Chosen Valley* (New York, 1948), for material on Fillmore County.

8   Blegen, *Norwegian Migration*, p. 312.

9   Soltow, *Toward Income Equality*, pp. 20, 21.

10   Letter to the author from Denmark's Nationalbank Sekretariat.

11   S. N. Procopovitch, "The Distribution of National Income," *Economic Journal* (March, 1926), p. 81; *Parliamentary Accounts and Records, 1801—02*, IV, 152—155, pp. 4—7.

CHAPTER 6

1   U.S. Census Office. 10th Census, 1880. Vol. VII, *Report on Valuation, Taxation, and Public Indebtedness in the United States* (GPO: Washington, D.C., 1884), pp. 12, 13, 16.

2   Willford King, *Wealth and Income of the People of the United States* (New York, 1915), p. 76, as adapted from a manuscript study by Max Lorenz, "The Distribution of Wealth in Six Wisconsin Counties" (Dane, Grant, Manitowoc, Milwaukee, Racine, and Winnebago).

3   U.S. Census Office. 12th Census, 1900. Vol. IV, *Vital Statistics* (GPO: Washington, D.C., 1902), Pt. 2, "Statistics of Deaths," p. 660; U.S. Census Office. 12th Census, 1900. Vol. II, *Population* (GPO: Washington, D.C., 1902), Pt. 2, "Ages, . . . ," pp. 106, 107, 209, 210.

4   For reported estates in 1936, $N = 3,859$; $\bar{X} = \$17,800$; and $R = 0.617$. The counterparts to these for 1927—1928 were 3,315; \$20,600; and 0.628.

5   The technique used at this point will be employed to much greater advantage in the next chapter with income data which encompass a much greater per cent of the labor force. The 1.6 per cent growth rate is obtained by considering that the number of deaths of males and females 45 and older in 1963 was 1.82 times that in 1927. Using an L_X of 1,000 in 1927 and 1,820 in 1963 in the above equa-

tions gives implied lower limits of $17,000 in 1927 and $54,700 in 1963.

The implied mean is related to the lower limit by (Lower limit)/ $(1-b) = \overline{X}$. This is for the case of a continuous distribution with an inverse Pareto slope of b. This leads to:

Year	Slope b	L_X	Implied lower limit	Implied $LL = \overline{X}$ $(1-b)$	Consumer price index	X in 1927 prices
1927	.683	1,000	$17,000	$ 53,600	1.00	$53,600
1963	.659	1,820	$54,700	$161,000	1.77	$91,000

and to $91,000 = $53,600 (1.016)^{36}$.

6 One may engage in calculations based on the technique described in the preceding footnote. The implicit mean in 1963 is $7,800, using the 18,000 deaths of those 50 and over in Wisconsin in 1962 in the calculation of the lower limit. The implicit means of those 50 and over in Wisconsin in 1860 and 1850 are $2,530 and $1,440. These three averages in 1860 dollars are $2,250 and $2,530 in 1963 and 1860, and $2,000 in 1850 if we adjust the 1850 average upward by 25 per cent to account for personal estate. The implication is that there has been no real growth.

The actual means of those 50 and over were $2,270 in 1860 and $904 in 1850. Drs. John Lansing and John Sonquist list mean net worth in 1962 as $14,600 per spending unit in the United States with those 50 and older having a mean between $11,900 and $16,900. Assuming a value in Wisconsin for those 50 and older in 1963 of twice the implicit mean signifies that average wealth only doubled in a 103- to 113-year period for an implicit average annual change of 0.7 per cent. Mean gross worth in 1960 in the United States was roughly two and one half to three times average wealth in 1860 in Wisconsin, giving an implicit average annual change of 0.9 to 1.1 per cent. This might be considered a maximum bound.

The Michigan group lists Gini coefficients of net worth of 0.69, 0.64, and 0.62 for age groups 35−44, 45−54, and 55−64 in 1962, and 0.69, 0.67, and 0.64 for age groups 25−34, 35−44, and 45−54 in 1953. In 1860, the Gini coefficients were 0.83, 0.71, 0.65, 0.72, and 0.70 for age groups 20−29, 30−39, 40−49, 50−59, and 60−69. One has the impression that per capita personal wealth has not increased as rapidly as income in the century and that inequality is about the same now as 100 years ago.

See John B. Lansing and John Sonquist, "A Cohort Analysis of Changes in the Distribution of Wealth," Conference on Research in Income and Wealth, National Bureau of Economic Research, March, 1967 (Mimeographed); and U.S. Bureau of the Census, *Statistical Abstract of the United States: 1963* (Washington, D.C., 1963), p. 345.

7   The censuses of manufacturing and agriculture for Wisconsin show
    a pronounced change from 1880 to 1890, as shown by the following
    data:

	1850	1860	1870	1880	1890	1900	1910
No. of farms/ No. of males 20 & older	0.24	0.34	0.39	0.38	0.31	0.29	0.25
No. of males 16 & older in manufacturing/ No. of males 20 & older	0.07	0.07	0.15	0.14	0.22	0.20	0.25
Difference	0.17	0.27	0.24	0.24	0.09	0.09	0.00

8   Net worth data for the United States for 1962 from Lansing and
    Sonquist, "A Cohort Analysis," pp. 6a and 11c, indicate an implicit
    growth rate of 1.8 per cent a year using net worth averages for five
    age classes between approximately 30 and 75. The study by Dorothy S. Projector and Gertrude S. Weiss for 1962 in the United
    States, in *Survey of Financial Characteristics of Consumers*,
    Federal Reserve Technical Papers (Washington, 1966), pp. 110,
    151, has a population-weighted r of 3.1 per cent for consumer
    units, with the head being of adult age.

9   In the Wisconsin census of occupations of 1860, there are reported
    31,472 farm laborers and 93,859 farmers for a total of 125,331.
    With 68,782 farms reported, we are left with 56,549 individuals
    presumably without farms. There is still another group, perhaps
    not large, of farm sons 20 and over, living on farms, whose occupation was not listed.

10 Lee Soltow, *Toward Income Equality in Norway* (Madison, 1965),
    p. 15.

11 Witt Bowden, Michael Karpovich, and Abbott Payson Usher, *An
    Economic History of Europe Since 1850* (New York, 1937), pp.
    282—83.

12 P. G. Craigie, "The Size and Distribution of Agricultural Holding
    in England and Abroad," *Journal of the Royal Statistical Society*
    (March, 1887). A distribution of German landholdings above 0.2
    hectares, or half an acre, has an $R = 0.74$. Above 1 hectare it is
    0.66. No allowance is made for farm laborers.

CHAPTER 7

1   A general idea of the definition of income may be obtained by examining an income tax return similar to that in G. S. Boutwell,
    The Taxpayer's Manual (1866), p. 156. Taxable income included
    all interest received on notes, bonds, and mortgages less interest

paid; income from partnerships, rents, and dividends. Rent of the dwelling where the taxpayer lived was deductible as was produce raised for home consumption. Expenses connected with renting land were deductible, including hired labor, repairs, and worthless debt (but not depreciation). Salaries and payments from the United States government were not taxable. See also J. B. Hill, "The Civil War Income Tax," *Quarterly Journal of Economics*, 8 (1894); and Rufus S. Tucker, "The Distribution of Income Among Taxpayers in the United States, 1863—1935," ibid., 52 (1938).

2   For a continuous inverse-Pareto curve of the form $Y = aL_Y^{-b}$, $a \leq Y \leq \infty$, it can be shown that $\overline{Y} = a/(1 - b)$ and $R = b/(2 - b)$. See Lee Soltow, "The Share of Upper Income Groups in Income," *Review of Economics and Statistics* (Nov., 1965).

3   The data have not been introduced because of certain weaknesses discussed earlier. However, the Pareto curve in 1860 prices for 1913 is $X = \$282 \, N_X^{0.596}$. The coefficient 0.596 fits nicely between the 1864 and 1929 coefficients of 0.711 and 0.568. Furthermore, the implied arithmetic mean of \$693 leads to an implied growth rate from 1913 to 1929 of 2.05 per cent, the same rate as the implied rate from 1864 to 1929.

4   Frederick Merk has stated that the Great Lakes were closed one third of the year. See Merk, *Economic History of Wisconsin During the Civil War Decade* (Madison, 1916), p. 383.

5   The number of classes considered above \$1,000 and \$2,000 were 19 and 18 in 1916, 25 and 24 from 1917 to 1943, 17 and 16 from 1945 to 1950, 15 and 14 in 1959, and 19 and 18 in 1962.

6   Data for the United States pertaining to this issue are analyzed in Lee Soltow, "Shifts in Factor Payments and Income Distribution," *American Economic Review* (June, 1959). See also the important work of Frank A. Hanna, Joseph A. Pechman, and Sidney M. Lerner, *Analysis of Wisconsin Income*, vol. 9, *Studies in Income and Wealth* (New York, 1948), pp. 71, 72, 91.

APPENDIX 1

1   U.S. Census Office. 8th Census, 1860. *Instructions to U.S. Marshals* (GPO: Washington, D.C., 1860), pp. 13—16, in the American Philosophical Society Library, Philadelphia.

APPENDIX 2

1   One of the 27 individuals had no reported wealth. For the logarithmic transformation, he was assumed to have wealth of \$100.

Index